LAW OF HIGHER EDUCATION

FOURTH EDITION

VOLUME 2 INDEX

KAPLIN / LEE

prepared for
Capella University

WILEY

CUSTOM SERVICES

Bicentennial Logo Design: Richard J. Pacifico

To order books or for customer service, please call 1(800)-CALL-WILEY (225-5945).

Printed in the United States of America.

ISBN 978-0-470-89810-9

10 9 8 7 6 5 4 3 2 1

The Law of
Higher Education

A Comprehensive Guide to
Legal Implications of Administrative
Decision Making

VOLUME II

FOURTH EDITION

JOSSEY-BASS
A Wiley Imprint
www.josseybass.com

Published by Jossey-Bass
A Wiley Imprint
989 Market Street, San Francisco, CA 94103-1741   www.josseybass.com

Jossey-Bass books and products are available through most bookstores. To contact Jossey-Bass directly call our Customer Care Department within the U.S. at 800-956-7739, outside the U.S. at 317-572-3986, or fax 317-572-4002.

Jossey-Bass also publishes its books in a variety of electronic formats. Some content that appears in print may not be available in electronic books.

ISBN-10: 0-7879-8656-9
ISBN-13: 978-0-7879-8656-8

Library of Congress Cataloging-in-Publication Data

Kaplin, William A.
   The law of higher education / William A. Kaplin, Barbara A. Lee. — 4th ed.
      v. cm.
   Includes bibliographical references and index.
   Contents: Overview of higher education law—Legal planning and dispute resolution—The college and its trustees and officers—The college and its employees—Nondiscrimination and affirmative action in employment—Faculty employment issues—Faculty academic freedom and freedom of expression—Rights and responsibilities of individual students—Rights and responsibilities of student organizations and their members—Local governments and the local community—The college and the state government—The college and the federal government—The college and the education associations (on website)—The college and the business/industrial community (on website).
   ISBN-10: 0-7879-8659-3 (cloth)
   ISBN-13: 978-0-7879-8659-9 (cloth)
   1. Universities and colleges—Law and legislation—United States. 2. School management and organization—Law and legislation—United States. 3. Universities and colleges—United States—Administration. I. Lee, Barbara A. II. Title.
   KF4225.K36 2006
   344.73'074—dc22
                                        2006010076

Printed in the United States of America
FIRST EDITION
HB Printing   10 9 8 7 6 5 4 3 2 1

Statute Index

United States Constitution:
Art. I, § 8, cl. 1, 1299, 1301;
Art. I, § 8, cl. 3, 1268, 1301;
Art. I, § 8, cl. 8, 1334, 1355;
Art. I, § 8, cl. 17, 27;
Art. I, § 10, 735;
Art. I, § 10(1), 272;
Art. III, 96;
Art. IV, § 1, 119, 405n;
Art. VI, para. 2, 836;
Amend. 1, 23, 30, 53, 55–58,
  61, 63–66, 69, 71–73, 94, 103,
  127, 129–130, 219, 229, 233,
  244, 248, 272, 282–287,
  290–292, 300, 308–309,
  329–330, 338, 341, 422–423,
  435, 436, 453, 457, 459,
  461–462, 485, 487, 489, 498,
  509, 529, 535, 552, 565, 588,
  605–612, 613–615, 617–622,
  624–625, 627, 628–632, 634,
  636–637, 640, 642, 645–647,
  648, 653, 655, 657, 659–663,
  665, 666, 667, 669, 671–672,
  675, 677–679, 682–683, 685,
  687–691, 694–695, 698,
  706–708, 711–713, 714, 716,
  738–743, 841, 867–873, 878,
  890, 900–901, 912, 914, 922,
  944–945, 964, 994–998, 1000,
  1002–1004, 1006, 1008,
  1011–1012, 1013, 1015–1017,
  1019–1028, 1038–1039,
  1050–1055, 1057–1060, 1062,
  1064, 1068n, 1069–1070,
  1073–1075, 1078, 1082–1083,
  1086, 1097–1098, 1100–1104,
  1106–1108, 1112, 1114,
  1119–1121, 1170, 1203–1204,
  1210–1217, 1219–1224, 1227,
  1229–1234, 1236, 1238–1243,
  1264–1268, 1270–1272,
  1276, 1317, 1350, 1354,
  1370, 1384, 1386–1387,
  1389–1397, 1430–1432,
  1444–1445, 1448–1449, 1461,
  1548, 1660;
Amend. 4, 257, 268–269,
  612–613, 621, 741,
  861–866, 867n, 912, 1097,
  1142–1147, 1207–1208,
  1210, 1387;
Amend. 5, 269, 453–454, 914,
  1086, 1175, 1215, 1228, 1439;
Amend. 10, 1297, 1302;
Amend. 11, 97, 123, 192, 226,
  231–239, 249, 316–317, 353,
  384, 391, 399, 403, 409, 819,
  844, 960, 1216, 1298,
  1307–1312, 1335, 1351, 1361,
  1367, 1373–1374, 1405,
  1498, 1500;
Amend. 13, 1305;
Amend. 14, 30, 45n, 51, 54–55,
  60–61, 67, 69, 92, 97, 117,
  123, 233, 244, 317, 352–354,
  356, 384, 403–404, 426, 437,
  443, 445, 447, 490, 498,
  529–530, 534, 547, 549, 561,
  568, 588–591, 593, 606n,
  617–618, 649, 687–688, 753,
  758, 763, 767, 778, 782, 786,
  789, 791, 795, 805, 826, 830,
  833, 837, 854, 892, 922, 939,
  956, 959, 973n, 974, 981, 982,
  984, 1065–1066, 1086, 1125,
  1128, 1142, 1181, 1205, 1215,
  1220–1221, 1244, 1263, 1270,
  1289–1290, 1300, 1304–1307,
  1309–1311, 1351–1352, 1360,
  1367, 1383, 1451–1453, 1464,
  1475, 1499–1500, 1563, 1615;
Amend. 15, 1307, 1309;
Amend. 16, 1301;
Amend. 26, 38, 726, 1199,
  1202

Act to Incorporate Howard
  University, 27–28
Administrative Dispute Resolution
  Act of 1996, 1505
Administrative Procedure Act
  (APA), 1440–1441, 1503
Age Discrimination Act of 1975,
  121, 776–777, 819–820,
  858–859, 1469–1471:
  1474–1477, 1490n,
  1493–1501
Age Discrimination in Employment Act (ADEA), 298, 364,
  373, 399–403, 404, 432–433,
  456n, 482n, 516, 517:
  §4(d), 300;
  §4(f)(1), 400;
  § 4(f)(2), 432;
  § 4(l)(3)(B), 432–433;
  §14(b), 401

American Competitiveness and
  Workforce Improvement Act
  of 1998 (ACWIA), 318n
American Jobs Creation Act of
  2004, 1416
Americans With Disabilities Act
  (ADA) of 1990, 313, 325, 357,
  373, 391–399, 425–430,
  515–516, 768, 773–775,
  876 925–927, 960–962,
  1381–1384:
    Title I, 391–394, 1306;
    Title II, 394, 773, 807, 819,
      1141–1142, 1306–1307,
      1381–1383;
    Title III, 773, 819, 1096,
      1141–1142, 1382–1383,
      1577–1581;
    §102, 269
Animal Enterprise Protection Act
  of 1992, 1328–1329
Animal Welfare Act (AWA), 1325
Anticybersquatting Consumer Pro-
  tection Act (ACPA), 1366, 1389
Anti-Kickback Act, 1659
Architectural Barriers Act of 1968,
  1384, 1466n
Armed Services Procurement
  Act, 1424
Arms Export Control Act, 1334,
  1394

Bankruptcy Code, 1313,
  1553–1554:
    Chapter 7, 842–843, 847;
    Chapter 13, 842–843, 847
Bank Secrecy Act of 1970, 1333
Bayh-Dole Act, 1358–1359
Byrd Amendment, 1427–1428

Cable Act, 1332
Campus Sex Crimes Prevention
  Act (CSCPA), 888, 1032
Child Online Protection Act
  (COPA), 1388–1389
Child Pornography Prevention Act
  of 1996 (CPPA), 1388
Children's Online Privacy
  Protection Act of 1998, 1389
Civil Monetary Penalty Act
  (CMPA), 1401
Civil Rights Act of 1866, 390:
    § 1981. See United States Code,
      Title 42, § 1981
Civil Rights Act of 1871:
    § 1983. See United States Code,
      Title 42, § 1983
Civil Rights Act of 1964:
    Title II, 874;
    Title VI, 54, 749, 758, 782–783,
      820–823, 856, 1450–1462,
      1474–1477, 1483, 1488–1489,
      1490n, 1493–1501,
      1574–1577;

Title VII, 54, 121, 246n,
  298–301, 318, 373, 374–383,
  385, 387–388, 390, 406–410,
  411–413, 414–419, 420–424,
  433–435, 436–439, 445–449,
  510–512, 517, 522–526, 943;
    § 601, 1497–1498;
    § 602, 1498;
    § 702(a), 456–459, 462;
    § 702(e)(2), 457–458;
    § 703, 379, 446, 456;
    § 703(e)(1), 458;
    § 703(e)(2), 462;
    § 703(j), 445;
    § 703(k), 381;
    § 706, 106n
Civil Rights Act of 1991, 373, 375,
  379, 381:
    § 102, 121
Civil Rights Attorney's Fees
  Awards Act of 1976, 123, 124,
  1500–1501
Civil Rights Remedies
  Equalization Amendment
  of 1986, 1497, 1498
Civil Rights Restoration Act
  (CRRA) of 1987, 396,
  891–892, 1067–1068, 1480
Clayton Act:
    §12, 1374
Clean Air Act, 1378–1380
Clean Water Act, 1378–1379
Clery Act, 885, 1436
Communications Act of 1934, 1384
Communications Decency Act
  (CDA) of 1996, 1387–1393:
    § 509, 874–876, 1389
Comprehensive Environmental
  Response, Compensation,
  and Liability Act of 1980
  (CERCLA), 1378
Computer Fraud and Abuse Act
  of 1986, 1385
Consolidated Omnibus Budget
  Reconciliation Act of 1986
  (COBRA), 312
Contract Disputes Act, 1425
Controlling the Assault of
  Non-Solicited Pornography
  and Marketing Act of 2003
  (CAN-SPAM), 1314
Copyright Act, 1334–1355:
    § 103(b), 1346;
    § 107, 1335–1336;
    § 110(1), 1342;
    § 110(2), 1342;
    § 512(a), 1349;
    § 512(c), 1349;
    § 512(h), 1349
Copyright Amendments Act, 1339
Copyright Remedy Clarification
  Act in 1990, 1351–1352
Crime Awareness and Campus
  Security Act, 885–888
Criminal Penalties for Copyright
  Infringement, 1346

Cyber Security Enhancement Act
  of 2002, 1386

Davis-Beacon Act, 1425
Debt Collection Improvement
  Act, 852
Digital Millennium Copyright Act
  (DMCA), 875–876,
  1347–1350, 1353, 1389
Digital Theft Deterrence
  and Copyright
  Damages Improvement Act
  of 1999, 1350
DREAM Act, 781, 840
Drug-Free Schools and Communi-
  ties Act Amendments of 1989,
  1434–1435
Drug-Free Workplace Act of 1988,
  267, 393, 1432–1434

Education Amendments of 1972,
  386–389, 414, 420–424:
    Title IX, 54, 121, 136, 376,
      439, 749–752, 762–768,
      782–783, 817–818, 820–823,
      856, 889, 892, 899, 943,
      945–954, 1127–1140,
      1462–1464, 1479–1482,
      1483–1484, 1484–1485,
      1490n, 1493–1501,
      1573–1574;
    § 106.31(c), 818;
    § 106.37(a)(1), 817;
    § 106.37(a)(2), 817;
    § 106.37(a)(3), 817;
    § 106.37(b), 817;
    § 106.37(b)(2), 818;
    § 408, 783;
    § 902, 388, 1480n
Education Amendments of 1976:
    § 412(a)(4), 818
Education Department General
  Administrative Regulations
  (EDGAR), 1428
Education for All Handicapped
  Children Act, 959
Electronic Communications
  Privacy Act (ECPA) of 1986,
  867n, 1385–1387
Emergency Planning and Commu-
  nity Right-to-Know Act
  (EPCRA), 1377–1379
Employee Retirement Income
  Security Act of 1974 (ERISA),
  311–313
Enhanced Border Security and
  Visa Entry Reform Act:
    § 501, 898n
Equal Access to Justice Act, 123,
  1072n, 1503
Equal Pay Act, 373, 376, 383–386,
  411, 420–424, 456n, 517
Equity in Athletics Disclosure Act
  of 1994, 420, 1123

Export Administration Act of 1979, 1334, 1394

Fair and Accurate Credit Transactions Act of 2003, 1376
Fair Credit Reporting Act (FCRA), 358–359, 1376
Fair Debt Collection Practices Act, 848
Fair Housing Act, 859–860, 1182–1183
Fair Labor Standards Act (FLSA), 258, 305–311, 314, 328, 383–384, 399, 1310–1311
False Claims Act (FCA), 328, 1401, 1404–1405, 1436–1438
Family and Medical Leave Act (FMLA) of 1993, 313–317, 413n, 428, 1306
Family Educational Rights and Privacy Act (FERPA), 212, 753, 812, 848, 867n, 876n, 925, 1029–1034
Federal Advisory Committee Act, 1502
Federal Arbitration Act (FAA), 137–138, 1597–1598:
§ 1, 274
Federal Food, Drug and Cosmetic Act, 1319
Federal Property and Administrative Services Act of 1949:
Title III, 1424
Federal Technology Transfer Act of 1986, 1657
Federal Trade Commission Act, 1368, 1375–1376
Federal Unemployment Tax Act (FUTA), 325–326, 1414
Foreign Intelligence Surveillance Act, 1332
Fraud by Wire, Radio, or Television Communications Act, 1394
Freedom of Information Act Amendments, 1506
Freedom of Information Act (FOIA), 1327–1328

General Education Provisions Act (GEPA), 1428
GI Bill, 1424
Government in the Sunshine Act, 1507
Gramm-Leach-Bliley Act, 815

Hazard Communication Standard, 303–304
Hazardous and Solid Waste Amendments of 1984, 1379
Health Insurance Portability and Accountability Act (HIPAA), 198, 889, 1401–1404

Higher Education Act of 1965, 814, 816, 885, 994, 1202, 1424, 1437–1438:
Title IV, 813, 1435–1436;
Part H, 1532–1533;
§ 103, 1435;
§ 104, 1435;
§ 485, 1435
Higher Education Amendments of 1992, 885, 1030
Higher Education Amendments of 1998, 402, 814, 1031n, 1032n, 1083–1084, 1555:
§ 112, 994;
§ 119, 1429;
§ 483(f)(1), 1429;
§ 489(b), 1432
Higher Education Facilities Act of 1963, 1424
Higher Education Technical Amendments of 1991, 850
Homeland Security Act of 2002, 1386

Illegal Immigration Reform and Immigrant Responsibility Act of 1996 (IIRIRA), 318n, 778–780, 839–840, 1331:
§ 641, 898n;
§ 641(c)(2), 899
Immigration Act of 1990 (IMMACT), 318n, 319
Immigration and Nationality Act of 1952, 836, 837, 1315:
§ 1101(a)(15)(F), 1262–1263
Immigration Reform and Control Act of 1986 (IRCA), 318–319, 410–411
Improving America's Schools Act (IASA) of 1994, 1031n, 1372
Individuals With Disabilities Education Act (IDEA), 926, 959
Individuals With Disabilities Education Improvement Act of 2004, 959
Internal Revenue Code (IRC):
§ 1–1563, 1406;
§ 25A, 1415;
§ 41, 1408;
§ 74, 1408;
§ 108(f), 1414;
§ 115, 1408;
§ 117, 1408;
§ 117(a), 1412;
§ 117(d), 1414;
§ 127, 1408;
§ 135, 1415;
§ 170(b)(1)(A)(ii), 1415;
§ 170(f), 1410;
§ 170(m), 1416;
§ 221, 1415;
§ 222, 1415;
§ 501(c)(3), 245, 1408–1410, 1415, 1422,1654;
§ 509(a)(3), 1413;

§ 511–514, 1416–1419;
§ 512, 1634;
§ 512(a)(1), 1418;
§ 512(a)(2), 1416n;
§ 512(b), 1635;
§ 512(b)(1), 1653;
§ 512(b)(1)(A)(ii), 1636;
§ 512(b)(2), 1417n, 1653;
§ 512(b)(3), 1417;
§ 512(b)(3)(A)(i), 1636, 1653;
§ 512(b)(3)(B)(i), 1636;
§ 512(b)(5), 1653;
§ 512(b)(6), 1418;
§ 512(b)(7), 1417, 1653;
§ 512(b)(8), 1417, 1653;
§ 512(b)(9), 1417;
§ 512(b)(13), 1418, 1654;
§ 512(c), 1417;
§ 512(e), 1418;
§ 513(a), 1417;
§ 513(a)(1), 1417n;
§ 513(a)(2), 1417, 1635;
§ 513(a)(3), 1417n;
§ 513(b), 1417;
§ 514, 1636;
§ 514(b)(1)(A), 1418;
§ 514(b)(1)(C), 1418;
§ 514(c)(9), 1418;
§ 529, 811–812, 1414;
§ 871, 1408;
§ 2001–2704, 1406;
§ 2055, 1415;
§ 2503(e), 1416;
§ 2522, 1415;
§ 3101–3501, 1406;
§ 3121(b)(10), 1413, 1414;
§ 3121(b)(13), 1413;
§ 3121(b)(19), 1413;
§ 3306(c)(10)(B), 1414;
§ 3306(c)(13), 1414;
§ 3306(c)(19), 1414;
§ 3309(b)(1), 1414n;
§ 4001–5000, 1406;
§ 4958, 1411;
§ 6033(a)(1), 1410, 1418;
§ 6050S, 1415;
§ 6104(e), 1410;
§ 7701(k), 1416
International Money Laundering Abatement and Anti-Terrorism Financing Act of 2001, 1333

Jacob Wetterling Crimes Against Children and Sexually Violent Offender Registration Act, 888

Labor-Management Relations Act of 1947 (Taft-Hartley Act), 279
Lanham Act, 1361–1368
Lobbying Disclosure Act of 1995, 1313

Local Government Antitrust Act of 1984, 1370

Military Selective Service Act, 1313
Miscellaneous and Technical Immigration and Naturalization Amendments (MTINA) of 1991, 318n
Morrill Act, 1424

National Competitiveness Technology Transfer Act of 1989, 1656
National Cooperative Research and Production Act of 1993, 1655, 1656
National Defense Education Act, 1424
National Labor Relations Act of 1935, 279–282, 283–286, 288, 289, 290, 293, 328, 491–496:
§ 8(b), 496
National Voter Registration Act (NVRA), 895, 1313, 1432
Need-Based Educational Aid Act of 2001, 1372
Negotiated Rulemaking Act of 1990, 1503–1504
No Electronic Theft Act (NET), 1347

Occupational Safety and Health Act (OSHA), 93, 261, 303–305
Office of Federal Procurement Policy Act of 1974, 1424
Older Workers Benefit Protection Act (OWBPA), 364, 401–402, 432–433
Omnibus Transportation Employee Testing Act of 1991, 267, 269

Patent Act, 1356–1361:
§ 271(a), 1652
Patent and Plant Variety Protection Remedy Clarification Act of 1992, 1360–1361
Patent and Trademark Amendments of 1980, 1655–1656
Pendleton Act, 275
Pension Reform Act, 311–313
Personal Responsibility and Work Opportunity Reconciliation Act (PRWORA), 839
Pregnancy Discrimination Act of 1978, 412
Privacy Act of 1974, 1040–1041, 1506–1507:
§ 3(m), 1041;
§ 7, 1041

Privacy Protection Act of 1980, 1208:
§101(a), 1208–1209;
§101(b), 1209;
§106, 1209
Program Fraud Civil Remedies Act of 1986 (PFCRA), 1405–1406, 1436–1437
Public Health Act, 1329
Public Health Security and Bioterrorism Preparedness and Response Act (BPARA) of 2002, 1333
Public Health Service Act Title X, 892, 1443–1445

Regulatory Flexibility Act, 1503–1504
Rehabilitation Act Amendments of 1992, 394–395
Rehabilitation Act of 1973, 925–927:
Title I, 894;
§ 503, 396, 444;
§ 504, 391–399, 429–430, 768–775, 818–819, 856, 876, 889, 893–894, 960–962, 1140–1142, 1312, 1464–1468, 1475–1477, 1485–1486, 1489, 1490n, 1493–1501
Religious Freedom Restoration Act (RFRA), 60, 285n, 890
Religious Land Use and Institutionalized Persons Act, 60n
Resource Conservation and Recovery Act of 1976 (RCRA), 1377–1380
Retirement Equity Act of 1984:
§ 102(e), 312;
§ 103, 312;
§ 104, 312
Robinson-Patman Act, 1368–1375, 1600–1601

Safe Drinking Water Act, 328
Sarbanes-Oxley Act, 1314
Semiconductor Chip Protection Act of 1984, 1650n
Senior Reserve Officers' Training Corps Act, 27
Service Contract Labor Standards Act, 1425
Sherman Act, 1081–1082, 1368–1375, 1566–1571, 1632–1633:
§ 2, 1570, 1571
Single Audit Act of 1984, 1427
Solid Waste Disposal Act (SWDA), 1380
Solomon Amendment, 1429–1432
Sonny Bono Copyright Term Extension Act (CTEA), 1354

Stevenson-Wydler Technology Innovation Act of 1980, 1656–1657
Student Loan Default Prevention Initiative Act of 1990:
§ 668.15, 852;
§ 1085, 850
Student Right-to-Know and Campus Security Act, 813, 1031n, 1122, 1435:
Title I, 1435
Superfund Amendments and Reauthorization Act (SARA):
Title III, 1377–1379
Superfund Law, 1378

Taft-Hartley Act, 279
Taxpayers' Bill of Rights 2, 1410–1412
TEACH Act, 1342–1344, 1389:
§ 110(2), 1343;
§ 110(f), 1344
Telecommunications Act of 1996, 1384:
Title V, 1387–1393
Toxic Substances Control Act, 328, 1379
Trademark Act of 1946, 1361–1368
Trademark Law Revision Act of 1988, 1362–1363
Trademark Remedy Clarification Act (TRCA), 1367
Tribally Controlled College or University Assistance Act, 27
Truth-in-Lending Act, 811

Uniformed Services Employment and Reemployment Rights Act (USERRA), 330–332
USA PATRIOT Act, 624, 1032, 1330–1334, 1385, 1394:
§ 210, 1386;
§ 212, 1386;
§ 217, 1386;
§ 416, 898n, 1331;
§ 505(a), 1387;
§ 507, 899;
§ 817, 1331;
Title III, 1333

Veterans Programs Enhancement Act, 331
Victims of Trafficking and Violence Protection Act of 2000:
§ 1601, 1032
Vietnam Era Veterans Readjustment Assistance Act of 1974, 330
Violence Against Women Act, 1303, 1304n

Wagner Act. *See* National Labor
 Relations Act of 1935
Wetterling Act, 888

United States Code:
 Title 5;
  § 552, 1327–1328, 1506;
  § 552(a)(1), 1426;
  § 552(b), 1506;
  § 552(b)(4), 1328;
  § 552(b)(5), 1328;
  § 552(b)(6), 1507;
  § 552a(m), 1041;
  § 552b, 1507;
  § 561 note, 1504;
  § 565, 1504;
  § 571(2), 1505;
  § 571(3), 1505;
  § 572(a), 1505;
  § 572(c), 1505;
  § 601(3), 1504;
  § 601(4), 1504;
  § 601(5), 1504;
  § 602, 1503;
  § 603, 1503;
  § 604, 1503;
  § 609, 1504;
  § 610, 1504;
  § 706, 1442;
  § 706(2)(A), 1443;
 Title 7;
  § 2132(g), 1325;
 Title 8;
  § 1101(a)(15), 835;
  § 1101(a)(15)(B), 837, 1315,
   1316;
  § 1101(a)(15)(F), 897;
  § 1101(a)(15)(F)(i), 897;
  § 1101(a)(15)(H), 1316;
  § 1101(a)(15)(H)(i)–(iii), 318;
  § 1101(a)(15)(J), 897, 1315,
   1316;
  § 1101(a)(15)(M), 837, 897;
  § 1101(a)(15)(M)(i), 897;
  § 1101(a)(15)(O), 319, 1316;
  § 1101(a)(15)(P), 319, 1316;
  § 1101(a)(15)(Q), 319, 1316;
  § 1151–1159, 1315;
  § 1182(a)(3)(C), 1317;
  § 1182(a)(3)(C)(ii), 1317;
  § 1182(a)(3)(C)(iii), 1317;
  § 1182(e), 1315;
  § 1182(j), 897;
  § 1184(n), 319;
  § 1227(a), 898n;
  § 1324a(a), 318;
  § 1324a(b), 318;
  § 1324b, 410;
  § 1372(a), 898n, 1331;
  § 1372(c)(2), 899;
  § 1621(a), 839–840;
  § 1621(c), 779;
  § 1621(c)(1)(B), 840;
  § 1621(d), 840;
  § 1623, 840;

  § 1623(a), 780;
  § 1641(b), 779n;
 Title 9;
  § 1, 274;
 Title 10;
  § 983, 1429–1432;
  § 983(d), 1429;
  § 2111a(a)–(c), 27;
  § 2111a(e), 27;
  § 2111a(f), 27;
  § 9315, 27;
 Title 11;
  § 362, 843, 847;
  § 362(a)(6), 847;
  § 362(b)(3), 1553;
  § 362(b)(14), 1553;
  § 362(d)(1), 843;
  § 523, 842;
  § 523(a)(8), 843–846;
  § 524(a)(2), 846;
  § 525, 847n;
  § 525(a), 1554n;
  § 541(b)(3), 1553;
  § 727, 842;
  § 1321–1323, 842;
  § 1324–1325, 842;
  § 1324, 843;
  § 1328(a), 843;
 Title 15;
  § 1, 1372;
  § 13c, 1374n, 1600–1601;
  § 33(1), 1370;
  § 34–36, 1370;
  § 36(a), 1370;
  § 44, 1375;
  § 45(a)(1), 1375;
  § 278k(a), 1657;
  § 278k(a)(2), 1657;
  § 278n, 1657;
  § 1114, 1362;
  § 1117, 1362;
  § 1122, 1367;
  § 1125(a), 1363, 1367;
  § 1603(7), 811;
  § 1681(b), 359;
  § 1681a(x), 359, 1376;
  § 2601(b)(2), 1379;
  § 2622, 328, 1380;
  § 3701, 1656;
  § 3702(5), 1656;
  § 3704(a)–(c), 1657;
  § 3705(a), 1657;
  § 3705(a)(1), 1657;
  § 3705(b)(1), 1657;
  § 3710(e), 1657;
  § 3710(e)(1)(C), 1657;
  § 3710(e)(1)(I), 1657;
  § 3710(e)(1)(J), 1657;
  § 3710a(a), 1657;
  § 4302, 1655;
  § 4305, 1655;
  § 6801(b), 815;
  § 6805(b), 815;
 Title 17;
  § 101, 1347;
  § 107, 1351;

  § 108(d), 1351;
  § 108(e), 1351;
  § 108(h), 1354;
  § 201(b), 1345;
  § 504(c), 1350;
  § 512(a)–(d), 875;
  § 512(c), 875;
  § 512(e), 875;
  § 512(f), 875;
  § 512(g), 875;
 Title 18;
  § 175(b), 1332;
  § 875(c), 1394–1397;
  § 1030(a)(1), 1394;
  § 1030(a)(5)(A), 1385;
  § 1030(a)(5)(A)(i), 1385;
  § 1030(a)(5)(A)(ii)–(iii), 1385;
  § 1030(a)(5)(B)(ii), 1394;
  § 1030(a)(5)(B)(v), 1394;
  § 1362, 1394;
  § 1465, 1393;
  § 1693–1699, 292;
  § 2251, 1394;
  § 2252, 1394;
  § 2252A, 1394;
  § 2252B, 1394;
  § 2252B(b), 1394;
  § 2256, 1394;
  § 2319(a), 1346;
  § 2319(b), 1346, 1394;
  § 2319(c)(1), 1394;
  § 2319(c)(2), 1394;
  § 2331, 1032;
  § 2332b, 1394;
  § 2332b(g)(5)(B), 1032;
  § 2510 *et seq.*, 1332;
  § 2511(1)(a), 1385;
  § 2511(1)(c), 1385, 1386;
  § 2511(1)(d), 1385;
  § 2511(2), 1385;
  § 2511(2)(a)(i), 1385;
  § 2511(2)(a)(ii), 1385;
  § 2511(2)(c), 1386;
  § 2511(2)(i), 1386;
  § 2701(a), 1385;
  § 2701(c), 1385;
  § 2701(c)(1), 1385;
  § 2702(a), 1385;
  § 2702(b), 1386;
  § 2702(b)(8), 1387;
  § 2702(c)(3), 1386;
  § 2702(c)(4), 1386;
  § 2703, 1386;
  § 2703(c), 1386;
  § 2709(b), 1387;
  § 2709(c), 1387;
 Title 20;
  § 1001(a)(5), 1554;
  § 1001(c), 1554;
  § 1011a, 994;
  § 1011a(a), 1083–1084;
  § 1011a(b)(2), 1084;
  § 1011i, 1429;
  § 1011i(a), 1429;
  § 1011i(e), 1429;
  § 1070a *et seq.*, 814;

United States Code: (*Continued*)
§ 1070b *et seq.*, 814;
§ 1070c *et seq.*, 814;
§ 1070d-31, 814;
§ 1070d-33, 814;
§ 1071 *et seq.*, 814;
§ 1078-2, 815;
§ 1078-3, 815;
§ 1082(a)(2), 1441;
§ 1087a *et seq.*, 815;
§ 1087aa-1087ii, 814;
§ 1087cc(4), 849;
§ 1091a(a)(1)-(2), 852;
§ 1091(r), 814, 1429;
§ 1092, 420;
§ 1092(a)(1)(L), 1435;
§ 1092(e), 1435;
§ 1092(e)(1)(A), 1122;
§ 1092(e)(1)(B), 1122;
§ 1092(e)(1)(C), 1122;
§ 1092(e)(1)(D), 1122;
§ 1092(e)(1)(E), 1122;
§ 1092(e)(1)(F), 1122;
§ 1092(e)(2), 1122;
§ 1092(e)(6), 1122;
§ 1092(e)(8), 1122;
§ 1092(f), 885;
§ 1092(f)(1), 888;
§ 1092(f)(13), 1436;
§ 1092(g), 1123;
§ 1092(g)(1), 1123;
§ 1094(a)(10), 814;
§ 1094(a)(23), 1202, 1432;
§ 1094(b), 1439;
§ 1094(c)(1)(A), 1435;
§ 1094(c)(1)(D), 1435, 1439;
§ 1094(c)(1)(F), 1435, 1436, 1439;
§ 1094(c)(2)(A), 1439;
§ 1094(c)(3)(A), 1435;
§ 1094(c)(3)(B), 1436;
§ 1094(c)(5)-(7), 1435;
§ 1097(a), 1406, 1437;
§ 1099a, 1260n;
§ 1099a-3, 1533;
§ 1099a(a), 1248n;
§ 1099a(a)(1), 1260n;
§ 1099a(a)(2), 1260n;
§ 1099b, 1556;
§ 1099b(a)(3)(A), 1555;
§ 1099b(a)(4), 1555;
§ 1099b(a)(5), 1555;
§ 1099b(a)(5)(J), 1555, 1556;
§ 1099b(a)(6), 1555;
§ 1099b(a)(7), 1555;
§ 1099b(a)(8), 1555;
§ 1099b(c)(5), 1555;
§ 1099b(c)(6), 1555;
§ 1099b(e), 1536;
§ 1099b(f), 1536–1538, 1542–1543;
§ 1232, 1426, 1428;
§ 1232b, 1425;
§ 1232g(a)(4)(A), 1030, 1033;
§ 1232g(a)(4)(B)(ii), 876n;

§ 1232g(a)(4)(B)(ii), 1030;
§ 1232g(a)(4)(B)(iv), 1402;
§ 1232g(b)(4), 1032;
§ 1232g(b)(6)(C), 1031n;
§ 1232g(b)(7), 1032;
§ 1232g(h), 1036;
§ 1232g(i), 1032n;
§ 1232g(j), 899;
§ 1232i(c), 783;
§ 1234i(2), 1428;
§ 1681(a)(1), 762, 1462;
§ 1681(a)(2), 1462;
§ 1681(a)(3), 386, 767, 1462;
§ 1681(a)(4), 1462;
§ 1681(a)(5), 762, 767, 1462;
§ 1681(a)(6)(A), 1462;
§ 1681(a)(6)(B), 1462;
§ 1681(a)(7), 1462;
§ 1681(a)(8), 1462;
§ 1681(a)(9), 818;
§ 1682, 1480n, 1489;
§ 1683, 1490n;
§ 1684, 768;
§ 1686, 856;
§ 1687, 1480;
§ 1688, 892;
§ 1994, 813;
Title 21;
§ 802, 1331;
Title 26;
§ 41, 1656;
§ 190, 1466n;
§ 401 *et seq.*, 311;
§ 410(a)(1)(B)(ii), 312;
§ 414(d), 312;
§ 529(b)(1), 812;
§ 792, 1466n;
§ 2415(a), 851;
§ 6402(d), 851;
Title 28;
§ 1331, 1440;
§ 1367, 97;
§ 1441, 97;
§ 1738, 119;
§ 2412(d)(1)(A), 1504;
§ 2412(d)(2)(B), 1504–1505;
Title 29;
§ 152(2), 279;
§ 152(3), 280, 289;
§ 152(11), 280, 289;
§ 152(12), 282n;
§ 157, 279;
§ 158(a), 280;
§ 158(a)(1), 288;
§ 158(a)(2), 288;
§ 158(a)(3), 288;
§ 158(a)(5), 294;
§ 158(b), 280, 496;
§ 158(b)(3), 294;
§ 158(d), 294;
§ 159(b), 288;
§ 163, 295;
§ 173(b), 296;
§ 203(x), 309, 1310;
§ 206(d)(1), 384, 421;
§ 207(o), 307;

§ 207(p), 307;
§ 213(a)(1), 306;
§ 213(a)(17), 306;
§ 216(b), 309, 1310;
§ 218, 306;
§ 254(a)(2), 311;
§ 255(a), 306;
§ 623, 400;
§ 623(f)(1), 400, 401;
§ 623(f)(2)(B)(ii), 433;
§ 623(f)(3), 401;
§ 623(h), 373;
§ 623(k), 402;
§ 623(l), 402;
§ 623(m), 402;
§ 626(d), 401;
§ 626(f)(1), 402;
§ 628(d), 300;
§ 631, 399;
§ 633(b), 401;
§ 653(b)(4), 304;
§ 654, 303;
§ 657(c), 304;
§ 665, 303;
§ 666, 303;
§ 667, 304–305;
§ 793, 444;
§ 794, 391–399, 1464;
§ 794a(a), 1493;
§ 794a(a)(2), 1480n, 1490n, 1498;
§ 794a(b), 1501;
§ 794c, 1489;
§ 1001 *et seq.*, 312;
§ 1001(b), 311;
§ 1002(1), 311;
§ 1002(2), 311;
§ 1002(32), 312;
§ 1052(a)(1)(B)(ii), 312;
§ 1144(a), 313;
§ 1144(b), 313;
§ 2601(b)(1), 317;
Title 31;
§ 3716(c)(3)(A)(i), 852;
§ 3730, 1404;
§ 3801(a)(6), 1406, 1436;
§ 3802, 1405, 1436;
§ 3803, 1405, 1436;
Title 33;
§ 1367, 1380;
Title 35;
§ 101, 1356–1357;
§ 102, 1356;
§ 103, 1356;
§ 200, 1359;
§ 201, 1359;
§ 202, 1359;
§ 202(a)(i)-(iii), 1359;
§ 202(c)(4), 1359;
§ 202(c)(7), 1359;
§ 202(e)(5), 1359;
§ 202(f), 1359;
§ 203, 1359;
§ 205, 1359;
§ 284, 1359;
§ 285, 1359;

Title 38;
§ 3001 *et seq.*, 814;
§ 3452, 1556;
§ 3675(a)(2), 1532;
§ 4212, 444;
§ 4212(a)(1), 444;
§ 4304(4)(A)(1), 330–330;
§ 4312, 331;
§ 4323, 331;
Title 39;
§ 601–606, 292;
§ 4121(a), 330;
Title 41;
§ 403(11), 1432;
§ 609(a)(1), 1425;
§ 701(b)(1), 1433;
§ 702(a)(1), 1433;
§ 702(a)(2), 1433;
§ 702(b)(1), 1433;
Title 42;
§ 262a, 1332;
§ 289b(b), 1329;
§ 292 *et seq.*, 850;
§ 296(6), 1554, 1556;
§ 296g, 767;
§ 300a-6, 1443–1445;
§ 300ee(d), 1442;
§ 706(8)(D), 1467;
§ 1320d-6, 1404;
§ 1395f(g), 1399;
§ 1395h, 1398;
§ 1395cc, 1397;
§ 1395cc(a)(1)(A), 1397;
§ 1395cc(a)(1)(F)(i), 1397–1398;
§ 1395cc(f)(1), 1289n;
§ 1395oo, 1398;
§ 1395oo(f)(1), 1398;
§ 1395ww, 1397;
§ 1395ww(d)(5), 1398;
§ 1396a(w)(1), 1289n;
§ 1973gg05(a)(2)(B), 895;
§ 1981, 332, 389–391, 404, 510–512, 760–762, 782–783, 820;
§ 1981A, 393;
§ 1983, 42, 102–103, 104n, 230–241, 332, 346–357, 436–437, 576n, 943, 956–957, 1033, 1464;
§ 1988, 123, 124;
§ 2000d-1, 1480n, 1489, 1493;
§ 2000d-2, 1490n;
§ 2000d-3, 1472;
§ 2000e(j), 433–435;
§ 2000e-2, 456;
§ 2000e-2(a), 374, 408, 433–435;
§ 2000e-2(e)(1), 374, 433–435, 458;
§ 2000e-2(e)(2), 433–435, 457–458;
§ 2000e-2(j), 445;
§ 2000e-2(k)(1)(a)(i), 381;
§ 2000e-3(a), 373;
§ 2000e-5(e), 381;

§ 2000e-5(k), 510;
§ 2000e-8(c), 461;
§ 2000bb-2(1), 60;
§ 2000bb-3(a), 60;
§ 2751 *et seq.*, 814;
§ 3604, 859;
§ 3607(b)(1), 1183;
§ 5851, 1380;
§ 6103(a)(4), 1489;
§ 6103(b), 776;
§ 6103(c), 776, 1472;
§ 6104, 1493;
§ 6104(b), 1480n, 1489;
§ 6104(e), 1493;
§ 6104(e)(1), 1501;
§ 6104(e)(2)(B), 1496;
§ 6104(f), 1496;
§ 6105, 1490n;
§ 6928, 1378;
§ 6971(a), 1380;
§ 7604(b), 1379;
§ 7604a, 1379;
§ 9607(a)(B), 1379;
§ 9610, 328, 1380;
§ 9659, 1379;
§ 12101–12213, 392n;
§ 12102, 1381;
§ 12102(2), 392n, 960;
§ 12102(a), 391;
§ 12111(8), 392;
§ 12111(9), 392;
§ 12111(9)(B), 430;
§ 12111(10), 393;
§ 12112(a), 392n;
§ 12112(d)(3)(B), 430;
§ 12131–12134, 1141;
§ 12131, 1381;
§ 12132, 392n, 1381;
§ 12181–12189, 1141;
§ 12181, 1382;
§ 12181(7), 1578;
§ 12182(a), 1577;
§ 12182(b)(2)(A)(i), 1579;
§ 12182(b)(2)(A)(ii), 1579;
§ 14071, 888;
§ 14071(j), 888;
Title 47;
§ 223(a)(1)(A), 1388;
§ 223(a)(1)(A)(ii), 1387;
§ 223(a)(1)(B), 1387, 1388, 1389–1390;
§ 223(a)(2), 1387, 1388;
§ 223(d), 1387, 1388, 1389;
§ 223(d)(2), 1388;
§ 223(e)(4), 1388;
§ 223(e)(5), 1391;
§ 230, 874–876;
§ 230(c), 1389;
§ 230(c)(1), 874;
§ 230(c)(2), 874;
§ 230(c)(2)(A), 875, 1389;
§ 230(e)(1), 875;
§ 230(e)(2), 875;
§ 230(f)(2), 874;
§ 230(f)(3), 874;
§ 231(a)(1), 1388;

§ 231(e)(6)(A), 1388;
Title 50;
§ 1861, 1332;
§ 1861(b)(2), 1332;
§ 1861(d), 1332

Uniform Commercial Code (U.C.C.):
§ 1-103, 1592;
§ 2-104, 1603;
§ 2-105, 1592;
§ 2-207, 1594;
§ 2-313, 1601;
§ 2-314, 1601–1602;
§ 2-315, 1601–1602;
§ 2-316(1), 1602;
§ 2-316(2), 1602;
§ 2-718(1), 1597

Federal Rules of Appellate Procedure:
Rule 38, 123
Federal Rules of Civil Procedure:
Rule 11, 123;
Rule 12(b)(6), 113;
Rule 23(a), 106, 108;
Rule 23(b), 106;
Rule 23(b)(3), 107;
Rule 26(b)(1), 107–108, 109;
Rule 26(b)(3), 110;
Rule 56, 113
Federal Rules of Criminal Procedure:
Rule 42, 126
Federal Rules of Evidence
§ 501, 109

Code of Federal Regulations:
Title 5;
§ 353.103, 331;
Title 7;
Part 1c, 1320;
Title 8;
Part 103, 898;
Part 104, 898;
§ 204.5(h)(2), 320;
§ 214.2(f), 898;
§ 214.2(h), 320;
§ 214.2(m), 898;
§ 214.2(o), 319, 1316;
§ 214.2(p), 319, 1316;
§ 214.2(q), 319, 1316;
§ 214.3, 898;
Title 9;
§ 2.31(c), 1326;
§ 2.31(d), 1326;
§ 2.31(e), 1326;
Title 10;
Part 745, 1320;
Title 14;
Part 1230, 1320;
Part 1275, 1329;
Title 15;
Part 27, 1320;
§ 120–130, 1334;

Code of Federal Regulations:
(*Continued*)
§ 730–774, 1334;
§ 738.2(d)(2), 1394;
§ 772, 1394;
§ 774, 1394;
Title 16;
Part 254, 1375;
§ 254.0(a), 1375;
Part 314, 815;
Part 316, 1314;
§ 433.2(d), 1376;
Part 600, 359;
Part 1028, 1320;
Title 20;
Part 501, 320;
§ 656.2, 320;
§ 656.21a, 320;
§ 1082(a)(2), 816;
§ 1681(a)(6)(A), 1067;
Title 21;
Part 50, 1319;
§ 50.20, 1319;
§ 50.23, 1323;
§ 50.25, 1323;
§ 50.25(a), 1323;
§ 50.25(b), 1323;
§ 54.1 *et seq.*, 1659;
Part 56, 1319, 1324;
§ 56.108–56.112, 1322;
§ 56.109(b), 1319;
§ 56.111(a)(1), 1319;
§ 56.111(a)(2), 1319;
§ 56.111(a)(3), 1319;
§ 56.111(a)(4), 1319;
§ 56.120, 1320;
§ 56.121(d), 1320;
§ 56.123, 1320;
Title 22;
§ 41.31, 319;
§ 41.53, 319;
§ 41.61, 898;
Part 62, 1316;
§ 62.9, 1316;
§ 62.20, 1316;
§ 121.1, 1394;
Part 225, 1320;
Title 24;
Part 60, 1320;
§ 60.102, 1320;
Title 26;
§ 301.6402-6(c)(1), 852;
Title 28;
Part 35, 1382;
§ 35.104, 965*n*;
§ 35.130(b)(1)(iii), 819;
§ 35.130(h)(7), 965*n*;
§ 35.140, 394;
§ 36.104, 819;
§ 36.202(b), 819;
Part 36.301, 1382;
§ 36.301-10, 773;
Part 36.302, 1382;
§ 36.302(a), 965*n*;
Part 36.303, 1382;
Part 36.304, 1382;

Part 36.305, 1382;
Part 36.306, 1382;
Part 36.307, 1382;
Part 36.308, 1382;
Part 36.309, 1382;
Part 36.310, 1382;
§ 36.401-6, 773;
Part 41, 1489;
Part 42, 1488;
§ 42.404, 1488;
§ 42.406, 1488;
§ 42.407, 1488;
§ 42.408, 1488;
§ 42.411, 1488;
§ 42.413, 1488;
§ 42.415, 1488;
Part 46, 1320;
§ 50.3, 1488;
§ 85.3, 1404;
Title 29;
Part 4, 1425;
Part 5, 1425;
§ 5.2(h), 1425;
Part 24, 1380;
§ 103.1, 279;
§ 103.30, 280–281;
Part 541, 306;
§ 541.202, 308;
§ 541.202(a), 306;
§ 541.202(a)(2), 306;
§ 541.300(a)(2), 306;
§ 541.301(e)(8), 307;
§ 541.303, 308;
§ 541.303(a), 306;
§ 541.303(d), 307;
§ 541.400(a), 307;
§ 541.602, 309;
§ 541.603(c), 310;
§ 541.710, 307;
Part 553, 307;
Part 825, 314;
§ 825.110(c), 314;
§ 825.113, 314;
§ 825.114, 315;
§ 825.204, 315;
§ 825.216–218, 315;
§ 825.301, 315;
§ 825.305–307, 315;
§ 825.310, 315;
§ 825.400-404, 315;
§ 825.500, 315;
§ 825.700(a), 315–316;
Parts 1600–1610, 374–375;
Part 1601, 375;
§ 1604.10, 412;
§ 1604.11, 414;
Part 1605, 434;
Part 1606, 409;
§ 1606.7, 409;
Parts 1620–1621, 385;
Part 1625, 401;
§ 1625.23, 402;
Part 1627, 401;
§ 1630, 393;
§ 1630.2(j), 397;
§ 1630.2(r), 394, 1467;

§ 1630.15(b)(2), 399;
§ 1630.21(j), 960;
§ 1641, 395;
§ 1910.1030, 304;
§ 1910.1200, 303–304;
§ 1910.1450, 304;
Part 2509, 312;
Part 2510, 312;
Part 2520, 312;
Part 2530, 312;
Part 2550, 312;
Part 2590, 312;
§ 2590.606, 312;
Title 31;
§ 500, 1334;
Title 32;
Part 26, 1432*n*;
§ 28.100 *et seq.*, 1428;
§ 216.3, 1429;
§ 216.3(b)(1), 1429;
§ 216.4, 1429;
Part 219, 1321;
Title 34;
Part 5b, 1041;
§ 5b.1 *et seq.*, 1507;
Part 21, 1505;
Parts 74–81, 1428;
§ 74.1(a), 1428;
§ 74.4(b), 1428;
§ 74.61, 1435;
§ 75.901, 1435;
§ 75.903, 1435;
§ 81.2, 1428;
§ 82.100 *et seq.*, 1428;
Part 84, 1434;
Part 85, 1438;
§ 85.105, 1438;
§ 85.200–85.220, 1438;
§ 85.811, 1438;
Part 86, 1434;
§ 86.100, 1434;
Part 97, 1321;
§ 99.1, 1029;
§ 99.1(d), 753;
§ 99.3, 753, 876*n*, 1030, 1036;
§ 99.5, 753;
§ 99.8, 1031;
§ 99.12, 753;
§ 99.30, 1033;
§ 99.31, 108*n*, 1031;
§ 99.31(a)(4), 812;
§ 99.31(a)(9)(iii), 1031;
§ 99.31(a)(13), 1031;
§ 99.31(a)(14), 1031;
§ 99.31(a)(15), 1032;
§ 99.32, 1032;
§ 99.34, 1033;
§ 99.37, 1030;
§ 99.61, 1029*n*;
§ 100.2, 1472;
§ 100.3(b)(1)–(b)(5), 856;
§ 100.3(b)(1), 1067;
§ 100.3(b)(2), 1474, 1497;
§ 100.3(b)(4), 1067;
§ 100.3(b)(6), 1471;
§ 100.3(b)(6)(i), 783;

§ 100.3(b)(6)(ii), 783;
§ 100.3(c), 1472;
§ 100.4, 1488;
§ 100.4(d), 856;
§ 100.5(i), 783;
§ 100.6(b), 1488;
§ 100.7, 1488;
§ 100.7(d), 1488;
§ 100.7(e), 1483;
§ 100.8, 1488;
§ 100.8(c), 1489;
§ 100.8(d), 1493;
§ 100.9, 1489;
§ 100.9(a), 1493;
§ 100.10, 1489;
§ 100.13(g), 1479;
Part 104, 1464–1467;
§ 104.3(j), 1465;
§ 104.3(k)(1), 395;
§ 104.3(k)(4), 965n;
§ 104.3(l)(1), 1465;
§ 104.3(l)(3), 768, 962, 1465;
§ 104.3(l)(4), 1465;
§ 104.4(b)(4), 1474;
§ 104.4(b)(5), 1474;
§ 104.6(a), 1471;
§ 104.6(b), 1471;
§ 104.6(c)(2), 1489;
§ 104.7(a), 1489;
§ 104.7(b), 1489;
§ 104.11, 395;
§ 104.12(a), 395;
§ 104.13(a), 395;
§ 104.13(b), 395;
§ 104.14(a), 395;
§ 104.22, 1466, 1467;
§ 104.37, 889;
§ 104.42(b)(1), 768;
§ 104.42(b)(2), 768;
§ 104.42(b)(3), 769;
§ 104.42(b)(4), 768, 769;
§ 104.42(c), 768;
§ 104.43, 889, 1465;
§ 104.43(a), 1479;
§ 104.43(d), 1466;
§ 104.44, 965n, 1466, 1467;
§ 104.44(d), 894;
§ 104.45, 856;
§ 104.45(a), 856;
§ 104.46(a), 818;
§ 104.46(a)(2), 818;
§ 104.46(c), 1465;
§ 104.47(a), 1140;
§ 104.47(b), 1466;
§ 104.47(c), 1466;
§ 104.61, 1483, 1493;
Part 104 App. A, 1140;
Part 106, 762, 1128, 1462;
§ 106.2(g), 1477;
§ 106.2(g)(1), 1478;
§ 106.2(h), 1478, 1573;
§ 106.2(n), 762;
§ 106.2(o), 762;
§ 106.2(p), 762;
§ 106.3, 1471;
§ 106.3(a), 783, 1471;

§ 106.3(b), 783;
§ 106.4, 1478;
§ 106.6(c), 1067;
§ 106.8, 1489;
§ 106.12, 386, 767;
§ 106.15(b), 762;
§ 106.15(d), 762;
§ 106.15(e), 762, 767;
§ 106.21–106.23, 762;
§ 106.21(b), 762–763;
§ 106.21(b)(2), 1474;
§ 106.21(c), 763;
§ 106.22, 763;
§ 106.23(b), 763;
§ 106.31, 1129;
§ 106.31(a), 1479;
§ 106.31(b)(6), 1067;
§ 106.32, 856, 1462;
§ 106.33, 856, 1462;
§ 106.34, 1129, 1462, 1474;
§ 106.36, 1462;
§ 106.37(b), 825n;
§ 106.37(c), 1129, 1139;
§ 106.38, 1463;
§ 106.39, 889, 892, 1463;
§ 106.40, 889, 892, 1463, 1474;
§ 106.41, 1129, 1139;
§ 106.41(a), 1139;
§ 106.41(b), 1129, 1130, 1139;
§ 106.41(c), 1130, 1139;
§ 106.41(c)(1), 1130;
§ 106.51–106.61, 386;
§ 106.51(a)(3), 1474;
§ 106.61, 386;
§ 106.71, 1483, 1489, 1493;
Part 110, 1469;
§ 110.10(a), 819;
§ 110.12, 819;
§ 110.13, 819, 1471;
§ 110.31, 1469;
§ 110.32, 1469;
§ 110.33, 1470;
§ 110.34, 1483;
§ 110.35, 1470;
§ 110.39, 1470
§ 361.47, 894;
Part 602, 1555, 1556;
§ 602.1, 1556;
§ 602.10, 1556;
§ 602.13–602.26, 1556;
§ 602.14(b), 1557;
§ 602.14(b)(2), 1557;
§ 602.15(a)(5), 1557;
§ 602.15(a)(6), 1557;
§ 602.18, 1557;
§ 602.18(a), 1557;
§ 602.18(b), 1557;
§ 602.21(c), 1560;
§ 602.22(c), 1556;
§ 602.23, 1560;
§ 602.23(c)(3), 1557;
§ 602.24, 1556;
§ 602.25, 1557;
§ 602.26, 1559;
§ 602.27(e)–(f), 1556;
§ 602.28, 1556;

§ 602.31(b)(2), 1556, 1557;
§ 602.31(b)(3), 1556, 1557;
§ 602.34–602.45, 1558;
§ 602.35(b)(1)(ii), 1556;
§ 602.36(c), 1556;
§ 602.45, 1558;
Part 603, 1556;
Part 654.1, 814;
Part 668, 812–813, 1122–1123;
§ 668.3, 813;
§ 668.8, 812;
§ 668.8(e), 813;
§ 668.14, 813;
§ 668.15, 851;
§ 668.19, 813;
§ 668.24, 816;
§ 668.37, 815;
§ 668.40, 814;
§ 668.46, 887, 1123;
§ 668.46(b)(12), 888;
§ 668.48, 1123;
§ 668.49, 1123;
§ 668.84, 1436;
§ 668.85–668.98, 1435;
§ 668.92, 1436;
§ 668.133, 816;
§ 668.136(c), 816;
Part 673, 814;
Part 674, 814;
§ 674.4, 850;
§ 674.41 $et\ seq.$, 849;
§ 674.41(a), 849;
§ 674.42(b), 849;
§ 674.42(b)(4), 849;
§ 674.42(c), 849;
§ 674.43, 850;
§ 674.46, 851;
§ 674.47, 851;
Part 675, 814;
§ 675(a), 850;
Part 676, 814;
Part 682, 814, 815;
§ 682.610(a), 850;
§ 682.713, 1435;
§ 688.185–668.198, 1435;
Part 690, 814;
Part 692, 814;
Title 36;
Part 1190, 1384, 1466n;
Part 1191, 1384, 1466n;
Title 38;
Part 16, 1321;
Part 21, 814;
Title 40;
Part 26, 1321;
Title 41;
Part 60-1, 443;
§ 60-1.1, 1425;
§ 60-1.4, 405;
§ 60-1.5, 405;
§ 60-1.5(a)(4), 406;
§ 60-1.5(a)(5), 406;
§ 60-1.7(a), 405;
§ 60-1.20, 406;
§ 60-1.21–60-1.24, 406;
§ 60-1.26(b)(2), 406;

Code of Federal Regulations:
 (*Continued*)
 § 60-1.27(b), 406;
 § 60-1.40, 443;
 Part 60-2, 443;
 § 60-2.1(d)(4), 406;
 § 60-2.10, 443;
 § 60-2.16, 443;
 § 60-2.16(e)(1), 443;
 Part 60-250, 444;
 § 60-250.21(f), 444;
 § 60-250.21(g), 444;
 Part 60-741, 444;
 § 60-741.21(f), 444;
 § 60-741.21(g), 444;
 Title 42;
 § 50.604–50.606, 1659;
 Part 57, 850;
 § 57.210(b), 850;
 § 57.215(c), 850;
 § 59.1–59.12, 892;
 § 59.5, 892;
 Part 60, 850;
 § 60.61, 850;
 Part 73, 1333;
 Part 93, 1329;
 § 93.103, 1330;
 § 93.224, 1330;
 § 93.226, 1330;
 § 93.307, 1330;
 § 93.308, 1330;
 § 93.310, 1330;
 § 93.311, 1330;
 § 93.313, 1330;
 § 93.315, 1330;
 § 93.413, 1330;
 Part 121, 1333;
 Part 331, 1333;
 § 412.2(f)(2), 1398;
 § 412.2(f)(7), 1398;
 § 412.105, 1398;
 § 413.75 *et seq.*, 1398;
 § 413.75–413.83, 1400, 1401;
 § 413.75, 1399;
 § 413.17(a), 1398;
 § 413.81(a)(1), 1399;
 § 413.85, 1398;
 § 413.85(c), 1399;
 § 413.86, 1401;
 § 413.86(e), 1400;
 § 413.90(a), 1398;
 Title 45;
 Part 46, 1319, 1321, 1324;
 § 46.102, 1321;
 § 46.109(b), 1319;
 § 46.111(a)(1), 1319;
 § 46.111(a)(2), 1319;
 § 46.111(a)(3), 1319;
 § 46.111(a)(4), 1319;
 § 46.116, 1319;
 Part 90, 776, 1469;
 § 90.2(a), 1469;
 § 90.3(a), 1479;
 § 90.3(b)(2), 1472;
 § 90.12, 1474;
 § 90.14, 776;

 § 90.15, 777;
 § 90.31, 1489;
 § 90.41–90.50, 1493;
 § 90.44(a), 1489;
 § 90.47(b), 1480*n*, 1489;
 § 90.49, 1472;
 § 90.50, 1496;
 Part 91, 1469;
 § 91.45, 1483;
 Part 160, 1402;
 § 160.103, 1402, 1403;
 Part 164, 1402;
 § 164.501, 1402;
 § 164.502(e), 1402;
 § 164.504(a)–(c), 1403;
 § 164.504(e), 1402;
 § 164.530(a)(1), 1403;
 § 164.530(b), 1403;
 § 164.530(d)(1), 1403;
 Part 689, 1329;
 § 689.2(c), 1330;
 Part 690, 1321;
 Title 48;
 § 3.104–3.111, 1425;
 § 9.104-1(d), 1425;
 § 16.1–16.7, 1425;
 § 22.300 *et seq.*, 1425;
 § 49.101(b), 1425;
 Part 203, 1659;
 § 235.017(a)(2), 1659;
 § 324.70, 713;
 § 352.224-70, 713;
 § 909.503–507.2, 1659;
 Title 49;
 Part 11, 1321;
 § 382.303, 269;
 § 382.305, 269;
 § 382.309, 269;
 § 382.311, 269;
 § 382.605, 269

State statutes:
 Alabama:
 Alabama Code;
 § 16-1-28(a), 1054;
 § 16-1-28(b), 1054;
 Alaska:
 Alaska Human Rights
  Act, 440;
 Arizona:
 Arizona Revised Statutes;
 § 13-1093, 883;
 § 13-1982, 883;
 § 15-442(A)(16), 884;
 § 15-679(A)(3), 883;
 § 15-679(A)(9), 883;
 § 15-1637, 246;
 § 32-1401(25)(x), 1290;
 § 32-1854(45), 1290;
 § 36-2302, 1290;
 § 41-2751 *et seq.*, 1629;
 § 41-2753, 1629;
 § 41-2753(A)(2), 1629;
 § 41-2753(B), 1629;
 § 41-2753(C), 1629;
 § 41-2753(D), 1629;

 Arkansas;
 Arkansas Constitution;
 Amend. 68, § 1, 1289;
 Arkansas Code Annotated;
 § 6-63-104(a), 542;
 California:
 California Constitution;
 Art. I, § 1, 1145;
 Art. I, § 2, 1210;
 Art. I, § 13, 1210;
 Art. I, § 31(a), 791;
 Art. IX, § 6, 1607;
 Art. IX, § 9, 188, 1256;
 Art. XIII, § 3(a), 1187;
 Art. XIII, § 3(d), 1187;
 California Fair Employment
  and Housing Act, 376;
 § 12940, 425*n*;
 California Leonard Law, 1023;
 California Tort Claims Act;
 § 835, 884;
 California Proposition 209, 455,
  791;
 California Business &
  Professions Code;
 § 1260, 1532;
 California Code of Civil
  Procedure;
 § 1094.5, 577;
 California Education Code
 § 23604, 1164;
 § 23604.1, 1164;
 § 23751, 1164;
 § 32050, 1086, 1275;
 § 66010.8(a), 839–840;
 § 66301, 994;
 § 66400–66402, 1275;
 § 67381, 879;
 § 68062(h), 837–839;
 § 76120, 994, 1013;
 § 87100–87107, 455;
 § 87101(d), 455;
 § 92612, 705;
 § 94367, 994, 1023;
 California Government Code;
 § 820.2, 334;
 § 995 *et seq.*, 154;
 § 12940, 425*n*;
 § 19130, 1607;
 § 53060, 1607;
 § 53094, 1178;
 California Health & Safety Code
 Ch. 1.3, 1288;
 § 7054.4, 1288;
 California Penal Code;
 § 290(a)(1)(A), 1275;
 § 626.2, 1217;
 § 626.4, 1217, 1218;
 § 626.6, 1217, 1246;
 § 626.7, 1217;
 California Public Contract Code;
 § 3410, 1599;
 § 10500.5(a), 1615;
 § 10501, 1615;
 § 10503, 1612;
 § 10860, 1599;

California Administrative Code;
Title 5, § 4000 et seq., 1164;
Colorado:
Colorado Constitution;
Art. VIII, § 5, 243;
Art. VIII, § 5(1), 1258;
Art. VIII, § 5(2), 1258;
Colorado Revised Statutes;
§ 23-5-124, 1275;
§ 23-21-403(1)(a), 243;
§ 24-113-101 et seq., 1629;
Connecticut:
Connecticut Uniform Manage-
ment of Institutional Funds
Act, 181;
District of Columbia:
District of Columbia Nation's
Capitol Religious Liberty and
Academic Freedom Act,
1056n;
District of Columbia Non-Profit
Corporation Act, 177;
District of Columbia Self-
Government and Governmen-
tal Reorganization Act, 1056n;
Florida:
Florida Tort Claims Act, 192;
Florida Statutes;
§ 240.605, 1531;
§ 240.4022, 1531;
§ 240.5339–240.5349, 1564;
§ 468.454, 1122, 1275;
§ 468.4562, 1564;
§ 481.223, 1612;
§ 489.113, 1612;
§ 768.28, 192;
§ 768.075, 200;
§ 1006.63(2), 1086;
Florida Administrative Code
Annotated;
Rule 6C-6.002(7), 801;
Georgia:
Georgia Open Records Act,
1282;
Georgia Code Annotated;
§ 16-9-93.1, 868;
§ 45-10-23, 1660;
§ 45-10-24.1, 1660;
§ 45-10-25, 1660;
§ 45-10-26, 1660;
§ 45-10-40, 1660;
Idaho:
Idaho Code;
§ 54-2902(d), 1629, 1629n;
§ 63-3029A, 1532;
§ 67-2309, 1613;
§ 67-5711C, 1613;
Illinois:
Illinois Community College
Tenure Act, 484;
Illinois Governmental
Ethics Act, 1659;
Illinois University Credit and
Retail Sales Act, 1630;
Illinois Compiled Statutes;
Title 5, § 350(2)(d), 154;

Title 20, § 3110/0.01 et seq.,
1612;
Title 30, § 575/1 et seq., 1615;
Title 35, § 200/15-35, 1637;
Title 35, § 205/19.1, 1194;
Title 110, § 25/1 et seq., 1564;
Title 110, § 75/1, 1626n;
Title 110, § 100/1, 1659;
Title 720, § 120/5, 1122;
Illinois Revised Statutes;
Ch. 38, para. 81-26, § 6(1),
1289;
Ch. 144, para. 221, 1086;
Indiana:
Indiana Teachers Tenure Act,
479;
Indiana Code;
§ 6-3-3-5(d), 1532;
§ 10-4533, 1220;
Iowa:
Iowa Code;
Ch. 23A, 1630;
§ 23 A.2(2), 1630;
§ 23 A.2(10)(K), 1630;
§ 73.6, 1599;
§ 262.44, 1629;
§ 279.24, 594;
Kansas:
Kansas Act for Judicial
Review and Civil
Enforcement of Agency
Actions, 1287;
Kansas Statutes Annotated;
§ 76-711(a), 1287;
§ 76-729(c)(4), 831;
§ 76-731(a), 840;
Louisiana:
Louisiana Administrative
Procedure Act, 1287;
Louisiana Public Records Act,
247;
Louisiana Revised Statutes
Annotated;
§ 17:3361(A)(5), 1606;
§ 39:1551–1755, 1606;
§ 39:1556, 1606;
§ 42.1111C(2)(d), 1600;
§ 42.1112B(2), 1600;
§ 42.1112B(3), 1600;
Maryland:
Maryland Education Code;
§ 26-201, 1275;
§ 26-301, 1275;
Maryland Health Code;
§ 20-214(b), 1289;
Maryland State Finance and
Procurement Code;
§ 14-207(c), 1599;
Massachusetts:
Massachusetts Fair Educational
Practices Act, 777;
Massachusetts General Laws;
Ch. 40, § 3, 1178;
Ch. 41, § 98F, 887;
Ch. 75 App., § 1-18, 1614;
Ch. 93A, 1609–1610;

Ch. 112, § 52, 1275;
Ch. 151C, § 2(f), 1035;
Ch. 151C, § 2A(a), 763;
Ch. 231, § 85K (2002), 194;
Ch. 266, § 120, 1217;
Ch. 266, § 121A, 1217;
Ch. 266, § 123, 1217;
Ch. 269, § 17–19, 1086, 1275;
Michigan:
Michigan Employee
Right-to-Know Act, 704;
Michigan Compiled Laws;
§ 691.1408, 154;
§ 722.52, 726;
§ 750.411e, 1122, 1275;
Minnesota:
Minnesota Statutes;
§ 16B.17, 1607;
§ 137.35, 1599;
§ 336.2-104(1), 1603;
§ 363A.01 et seq., 1289;
§ 604.10, 1603;
Mississippi:
Mississippi Public Records Act,
1035;
Missouri:
Missouri General Not-for-Profit
Corporation Law, 175;
Montana:
Montana Code Annotated;
§ 20-25-302, 1630–1631;
§ 39-2-901 et seq., 1273;
Nebraska:
Nebraska Revised Statutes;
§ 81.15, 1599;
Nevada:
Nevada Revised Statutes;
§ 398.155 et seq., 1564;
§ 398.245, 1564;
§ 398.490, 1564;
New Hampshire:
New Hampshire Consumer
Protection Act, 178;
New Jersey:
New Jersey Act of 1909, 479;
New Jersey Act of 1933, 479;
New Jersey Charitable
Immunity Act, 194;
New Jersey Desert Storm
Law, 155;
New Jersey Domestic
Partnership Act, 441;
New Jersey Law Against
Discrimination, 425n,
440–441;
New Jersey Tort Claims Act,
155–156;
New Jersey Statutes Annotated;
§ 26:3D-17, 1274;
§ 40:55-39(d), 1177;
§ 52:13D-12-27, 1274;
§ 59:10A-1, 155;
§ 59:10A-2, 155;
§ 59:10A-4, 156;
New York:
New York Bundy Law, 1261;

State statutes: (*Continued*)
New York Freedom of Information Law (FOIL), 1328;
New York Standardized Testing Act, 1355;
New York State Human Rights Law, 860;
New York State Roommate Law, 860;
New York Agriculture and Markets Law, 1275;
New York Civil Practice Law and Rules;
Art. 78, 577–578;
New York Education Law;
§ 201, 1259;
§ 207, 1259;
§ 216, 1259;
§ 217, 1259;
§ 224(1)(a), 1275;
§ 224(2), 1275;
§ 236, 175;
§ 355(2)(m), 183, 877;
§ 376, 1612;
§ 6401, 1261;
§ 6450, 988;
North Carolina:
North Carolina Open Meetings Law, 1040;
North Carolina General Statutes;
§ 105-278.4, 1194;
§ 116-15, 1270;
Ohio:
Ohio Administrative Procedure Act, 1286;
Ohio Public Records Act, 704, 1038;
Ohio Revised Code Annotated;
§ 3333.38, 1275;
§ 3343.06, 184;
§ 3345.45, 1275;
§ 3354.161, 1615;
§ 4115.34, 1599;
Oklahoma:
Oklahoma Constitution;
Art. 6, § 31a, 1257;
Art. 13-A, 1257;
Art. 13-B, 1257;
Oklahoma Competitive Bidding Act, 1613;
Oregon:
Oregon Constitution;

Art. I, § 20, 442;
Art. XI0-F(1), 1625;
Oregon Revised Statutes;
§ 20.107, 124;
§ 183.480(1), 101;
§ 348.835, 1268;
§ 351.070(2)(a), 1626;
§ 351.070(2)(c), 1626;
§ 351.160(1), 1625;
Pennsylvania:
Pennsylvania English Fluency in Higher Education Act, 1274;
Pennsylvania Unfair Trade Practices and Consumer Protection Law, 848;
Pennsylvania Whistleblower Law, 1274*n*;
Pennsylvania Consolidated Statutes;
Title 18, § 7107, 1275;
Title 24, § 2502, 887, 1275;
Title 35, § 7602 *et seq.*, 1289;
Title 53, § 2181, 1164;
Title 71, § 646.1, 877;
Title 72, § 5020-204(a)(3), 1196;
South Carolina:
South Carolina Freedom of Information Act, 247;
South Carolina Code Annotated;
§ 1-23-360, 111–112;
§ 59-102-30, 1275;
§ 59-103-30 (2001), 542;
South Dakota;
South Dakota Codified Laws;
§ 10-4-9.2, 1190;
Tennessee:
Tennessee Code Annotated;
§ 49-8-304, 1288;
Texas:
Texas Tort Claims Act, 193;
Texas Education Code Annotated;
§ 4.30(a), 1275;
§ 4.30(b)(2), 1275;
§ 37.152, 914;
§ 51.803, 790;
§ 51.842(b), 1274;
§ 54.052(f), 828;
§ 54.054, 828;
§ 61.301–61.319, 1267;
Texas Penal Code Annotated;
§ 36.08, 1661;

Texas Revised Civil Statutes Annotated;
Art. 601b, 1599, 1612;
Utah:
Utah Higher Education Act of 1969, 172;
Utah Compiled Laws;
§ 1855, 172;
Vermont:
Vermont State Employee Labor Relations Act, 442;
§961(6), 442;
Vermont Statutes Annotated;
Title 1, § 317(c)(11), 1040;
Title 16, § 2282, 831;
Title 32, § 3001(c), 439;
Virginia:
Virginia Constitution;
Art. VIII, § 11, 1248;
Virginia Education Facilities Authority Act, 1248;
Virginia State and Local Government Conflict of Interests Act, 1660;
Virginia Code Annotated;
§ 2.2-2827(B) (2001), 659;
§ 2.2-3106(C)(7), 1660;
§ 2.2-3110, 1660;
§ 2.2-3120–3122, 1660;
§ 18.2-56, 1086;
§ 23-7.4:3(A), 832;
§ 182–423, 1020;
Washington:
Washington Revised Code;
§ 28B.10.814, 68;
§ 28B.63.010 *et seq.*, 1630;
§ 28B.101.040, 67–68;
§ 43.19.190, 1607–1608;
§ 49.60.400(1), 791;
West Virginia:
West Virginia Administrative Procedure Act, 1287;
West Virginia Code;
§ 5G-1-1–5G-1-4, 1612;
§ 18-29-1 *et seq.*, 275;
§ 29A-5-4(g), 1287;
Wisconsin:
Wisconsin Administrative Code;
§ UWS 17.01, 919;
Wisconsin Statutes;
§ 36.11(22), 1275;
§ 939.645(1)(b), 1020

Cases Index

A

A&M Records v. Napster, 1340, 1347–1348

Aase v. South Dakota Board of Regents, 579n

Aase v. State, 736

AAUP v. Bloomfield College, 580–581, 728

AAUP v. Central State University, 500

AAUP, University of Toledo Chapter v. University of Toledo, 139

Abalkhail v. Claremont University Center, 940–941

Abate v. Mundt, 1205

ABL Management, Inc. v. Board of Supervisors of Southern University and Agricultural & Mechanical College, 1605–1606, 1621

Abood v. Detroit Board of Education, 290, 1059

Ackerman v. Metropolitan Community College Area, 595

Ackerman v. President & Trustees of the College of Holy Cross, 991–992

ACLU Student Chapter v. Mote, 1224

Adair v. Troy State University of Montgomery, 1379–1380

Adamian v. Jacobson, 535

Adams v. Bell, 1452n, 1492

Adams v. Bennett, 1492

Adams v. Califano, 1451

Adams v. Richardson, 1451, 1491–1492

Adamson v. Wharton, 1660–1661

Adarand Constructors, Inc. v. Pena, 788, 796

Adelphi University, 495

Adelphi University v. Board of Regents of the State of New York, In re, 175

Ad-Hoc Committee of Baruch Black & Hispanic Alumni Association v. Bernard M. Baruch College, 243–244

Adler v. Board of Education, 620–621

Advent Systems, Ltd. v. Unysis Corp., 1592–1593

Advocates for the Arts v. Thomson, 1447

Agostini v. Felton, 62

Ahlum v. Administrators of Tulane Educational Fund, 989

Ahmed v. University of Toledo, 778, 834

Aievoli v. State University of New York, 557

Aimster Copyright Litigation, In re, 1348

Alabama; United States v., 1255

Alabama A&M University v. King, 309

Alabama State Teachers Association v. Alabama Public School & College Authority, 1452–1453, 1455

Alamo Foundation v. Secretary of Labor, 308

Albach v. Odle, 1116

Albany Medical College v. Lobel, 475–476

Albert v. Carovano, 46–47, 988–989

Albertini; United States v., 1005

Albert Merrill School v. Godoy, 734

Albertson's v. Kirkingburg, 961

Albright College, In re, 1186

Alcorn v. Vaksman, 930–931

Alden v. Maine, 239, 309, 1298, 1303–1304, 1310–1313, 1500

Alderson v. New York State College of Agriculture & Life Sciences, 1281–1282

Alexander v. Choate, 1475–1477, 1498

Alexander v. Gardner-Denver Co., 274, 299–300

Alexander v. Sandoval, 947n, 1135–1136, 1476–1477, 1483–1484, 1487, 1497–1498, 1576

Alexander v. Yale University, 943, 945–946

Alford v. Emory University, 1188–1189

Alicea v. New Brunswick Theological Seminary, 487–488

Alkhabaz aka Jake Baker; United States v., 869–870, 1395–1396
Allaire v. Rogers, 695–696
Allen v. Regents of the University System of Georgia, 1301
Allen; State v., 748, 1086
Allis-Chalmers Corp. v. Lueck, 293
Alpha Gamma Zeta House Association v. Clay County Board of Equalization, 1190
ALS Scan, Inc. v. RemarQ Communities, Inc., 1348–1349
Altschuler v. University of Pennsylvania Law School, 936–937
Alumni Association of the University of Oregon v. Commissioner, 1419n
American Asbestos Training Center, Ltd. v. Eastern Iowa Community College, 1630
American Association of Cosmetology Schools v. Riley, 1440, 1441, 1487
American Association of University Women v. Board of Trustees of the California State University, 839
American Bar Association; United States v., 1548n
American Civil Liberties Union v. Reno, 1389
American Civil Liberties Union of Georgia v. Miller, 868–869, 872–873, 1384n
American Future Systems v. Pennsylvania State University (618 F.2d 252), 1230–1232
American Future Systems v. Pennsylvania State University (688 F.2d 907), 1232–1234, 1236
American Future Systems v. Pennsylvania State University (752 F.2d 854), 1234
American Future Systems v. Pennsylvania State University (553 F. Supp. 1268), 1234
American Future Systems v. Pennsylvania State University (568 F. Supp. 666), 1234
American Geophysical Union v. Texaco, Inc., 1338–1339
American Hospital Association v. NLRB, 281
American International College, 494
American Library Association v. Pataki, 1272, 1384n
American Library Association; United States v., 1390n, 1391n
American Society for the Prevention of Cruelty to Animals v. Board of Trustees of the State University of New York, In re, 1280, 1328

American Society of Mechanical Engineers v. Hydrolevel Corp., 1370, 1547
Ames Contracting Co. v. City University of New York, 1605, 1612
Amherst College v. Assessors, 1186
Anderson v. Creighton, 349
Anderson; People v., 1086, 1122
Anderson v. University of Wisconsin, 805
Anderson v. Vanden Dorpel, 342
Andover Newton Theological School, Inc. v. Continental Casualty Company, 152–153
Andre v. Pace University, 215
Andrews v. Knowlton, 917
Animal Legal Defense Fund v. Espy, 1327
Animal Legal Defense Fund v. Institutional Animal Care & Use Committee of the University of Vermont, 1280, 1328
Animal Legal Defense Fund v. Madigan, 1325, 1327
Animal Legal Defense Fund v. Quigg, 1358
Anker v. G. D. Searle & Co., 711
Ann Arbor, City of v. University Cellar, 1193, 1639
Ansari v. New York University, 215
Anthony v. Syracuse University, 10, 988
Antioch University, In re, 178–179
Antonelli v. Hammond, 1107
Apex Hosiery Co. v. Leader, 1570
Apfel v. Huddleston, 209
Apollo Media Corp. v. Reno, 1388
Appalachian Student Housing Corp., In re, 1185–1186, 1631
Appeal of. See name of party
Application of. See name of party
Arabian American Oil Co.; EEOC v., 1484
ARA v. NLRB, 281
Arcadia Development Corp. v. Bloomington, 1176
Arenson v. Southern University, 512
Arista Records, Inc. v. MP3Board, Inc., 1349
Arizona v. Hicks, 865–866
Arizona Board of Regents v. Wilson, 754
Arkansas Educational Television Commission v. Forbes, 997, 998, 999, 1216
Arkansas Gazette Co. v. Pickens, 1277–1278
Arkansas Writers' Project, Inc. v. Ragland, 1448
Arlene Egelberg, In re Claim of, 327
Arlosoroff v. NCAA, 1562

Armstrong v. Accrediting Council for Continuing Education & Training, Inc., 853
Armstrong v. United States, 56
Arneson v. Board of Trustees, McKendree College, 470
Arneson v. Jezwinski, 350–351
Arnett v. Kennedy, 530
Arnold v. State, 1275
Aronson v. University of Mississippi, 809
Arriaga v. Members of Board of Regents, 735–736
Arrington v. Taylor, 1098
Arroyo v. Rosen, 339–340
Ashcroft v. ACLU (535 U.S. 564), 1389, 1390n
Ashcroft v. ACLU (542 U.S. 656), 1389, 1392n
Ashcroft; Doe v., 1387
Ashcroft v. Free Speech Coalition, 1388, 1394
Ashiegbu v. Williams, 980
Associated Press v. Crofts, 1278
Associated Press v. Walker, 1108n
Associated Students of the University of California at Riverside v. Regents of the University of California, 1058
Associated Subcontractors of Massachusetts, Inc. v. University of Massachusetts Building Authority, 1614
Association for Disabled Americans v. Florida International University, 1307
Association of Accredited Cosmetology Schools v. Alexander, 851
Association of American Medical Colleges v. Carey, 1355
Association of American Medical Colleges v. Cuomo, 1355
Association of New Jersey State College Faculties v. Dungan, 499
Atascadero State Hospital v. Scanlon, 1308, 1309, 1498, 1500
Atlanta College of Medical & Dental Careers, Inc. v. Riley, 1440
Atlantic Cleaners & Dyers v. United States, 1369
Atlantic Coast Conference, In re, 1194
Atlantic Community College v. Civil Service Commission, 1163
Auburn Alliance for Peace & Justice v. Martin, 1005, 1009–1010
Auburn University v. Advertiser Co., 1277

Auburn University v. Southern Association of Colleges & Schools, 1542, 1546

Auer v. Robbins, 309–310

Auerbach v. Rettaliata, 1200–1201

Avery v. Midland County, 1205

Avila v. Citrus Community College, 1152n

Avins v. White, 1550–1553

Axson-Flynn v. Johnson, 39, 653, 741–745

Ayers v. Allain, 1455, 1456

Ayers v. Fordice, 1460

Ayers v. Thompson, 1460n

Aymes v. Bonelli, 259

Ayoub v. Texas A&M University, 668, 671

B

Bair v. Shippensburg University, 1023–1024

Bakalis v. Board of Trustees of Community College District No. 504, 188

Baker v. Lafayette College, 572

Baker v. Southern University, 173–174

Bakke v. Regents of the University of California, 786, 798, 800, 821

Ballou v. Sigma Nu General Fraternity, 1090n

Bally v. Northeastern University, 1146

Baltimore, City of v. Poe, 1172

Baltimore Teachers Union v. Mayor of Baltimore, 478

Banks v. Dominican College, 937

Banks v. NCAA, 1569

Barazi v. West Virginia State College & the Board of Directors of the State College System, 276

Barbay v. NCAA & Louisiana State University, 1564

Bargstedt v. Cornell University, 577

Barham v. University of Northern Colorado, 482, 543

Barker v. Hardway, 1002

Barnes v. Gorman, 1383, 1497, 1498

Barran, Ex parte, 1094

Barrett v. Rosenthal, 875

Barrett v. University of Colorado Health Sciences Center, 1018n

Barrett v. University of Texas Medical Branch at Galveston, 329

Barrett v. West Chester University, 1136

Bartlett v. New York State Board of Law Examiners, 961

Bartlett, State ex rel. v. Pantzer, 755

Bartnicki v. Vopper, 1386

Basic Books v. Kinko's Graphics Corp., 1337

Bason v. American University, 37

Batcheller v. Commonwealth ex rel. Rector & Visitors of University of Virginia, 1622

Bates v. United States, 1406, 1437

Batzel v. Smith, 875

Bauer v. Dann, 210

Baughman v. Freienmuth, 1107

Baughman v. State, 879

Bayless v. Martine, 1004, 1005

Bazaar v. Fortune, 1101

Bazemore v. Friday, 519, 1454n

Beach v. University of Utah, 197

Bearman v. University of Notre Dame, 1212n

Beaulieu, State ex rel. v. Clausen, 1289

Beck v. Board of Trustees of State Colleges, 104, 576

Begel v. Wisconsin Labor & Industry Review Commission, 323

Begley v. Corporation of Mercer University, 1124

Behagen v. Intercollegiate Conference of Faculty Representatives, 1116

Behrend v. State, 1534n

Behrens v. Pelletier, 349

Beitzel v. Jeffrey, 553

Belle Terre, Village of v. Boraas, 1180–1181

Bellevue College v. Greater Omaha Realty Co., 1595–1596

Belliveau v. Rerick, 219

Bence v. Breier, 530

Bender v. Alderson-Broaddus College, 932

Bennett v. Wells College, In re, 541

Bennun v. Rutgers, The State University of New Jersey, 509–511, 529

Benson v. Allphin, 351

Bercovitch v. Baldwin School, 925–926

Berkowitz v. President & Fellows of Harvard College, 474–475

Berkshire School v. Town of Reading, 1184

Bethel School District v. Fraser, 630

Betts v. Rector & Visitors of the University of Virginia, 962

Beukas v. Fairleigh Dickinson University, 579n, 728–729, 731

Bexar Appraisal District v. Incarnate Word College, 1187

Bickerstaff v. Vassar College, 513

Bicknese v. Sultana, 345

Bidwell v. Zoning Board of Adjustment, 1177

Bienkowski v. Northeastern University, 311

Biggiam v. Board of Trustees of Community College District No. 516, 484

Bigler v. Cornell University, In re, 531

Billingsley, In re, 847

Billmyre v. Sacred Heart Hospital of Sisters of Charity, 263

Bilut v. Northwestern University, 807–808

Bingler v. Johnson, 1412n

Bird v. Lewis & Clark College, 971, 1485–1486

Bishop v. Aronov, 39, 611, 631–634, 644, 650, 653, 655, 1015

Bishop v. Texas A&M University, 207

Bishop v. Wood, 549–550

Bishop Ford Central Catholic High School; NLRB v., 284

Blackwell College of Business v. Attorney General, 1262–1263

Blair v. Board of Regents for the Oklahoma Agricultural & Mechanical College, 142

Blair v. Washington State University, 1128

Blair Academy v. Blairstown, 1192

Blake v. University of Rochester, 1152

Blanchard v. Lansing Community College, 173

Blank v. Board of Higher Education of the City of New York, 185, 934–935

Blanton v. State University of New York, 979

Blatt v. University of Southern California, 1529–1530

Bloch v. Temple University, 676

Bloss v. University of Minnesota, 206

Blum v. Schlegel, 642n, 649

Blum v. Yaretsky, 43, 1544

Board of Community College Trustees for Baltimore County—Essex Community College v. Adams, 586–587

Board of Control of Eastern Michigan University v. Burgess, 1593

Board of County Commissioners v. Umbehr, 1448–1449

Board of Curators, University of Missouri v. Horowitz, 131, 132, 592–593, 929, 983–985

Board of Education of Independent School District No. 92 v. Earls, 1144–1145

Board of Education of Rogers, Arkansas v. McCluskey, 924

Board of Governors of State Colleges & Universities; EEOC v., 300

Board of Governors of the University of North Carolina v. Helpingstine, 1363–1364, 1630

Board of Governors of Wayne State University v. Building Systems Housing Corp., 1593

Board of Regents v. Board of Trustees for State Colleges & Universities, 174

Board of Regents v. Carter, 142

Board of Regents v. Roth, 547–549, 551, 811, 983, 1118, 1584

Board of Regents of Higher Education v. Judge, 1253

Board of Regents of Kentucky State University v. Gale, 471

Board of Regents of Oklahoma State University v. Oklahoma Merit Protection Commission, 1257

Board of Regents of the Regency University System v. Reynard, 188, 248, 1279

Board of Regents of Universities & State College v. City of Tempe, 1165

Board of Regents of the University of Oklahoma v. Baker, 1257

Board of Regents of the University of the State of New York v. Tomanio, 102

Board of Regents of the University of Washington v. Frederick & Nelson, 1602

Board of Regents of the University of Wisconsin v. Dane County Board of Adjustment, 1168

Board of Regents of the University of Wisconsin v. Southworth, 648, 651n, 739–740, 1058–1065, 1098, 1238n

Board of Trustees v. City of Los Angeles, 1164, 1165

Board of Trustees v. Department of Administrative Services, 1286–1287

Board of Trustees for the University of Alabama; United States v., 770

Board of Trustees of Howard Community College v. John K. Ruff, Inc., 1253

Board of Trustees of Junior College District No. 508 v. Cook County College Teachers Union, 287

Board of Trustees of the Leland Stanford Junior University v. Sullivan, 1445

Board of Trustees of Ohio State University v. Department of Administrative Services, 595

Board of Trustees of Stanford University v. Sullivan, 623, 713

Board of Trustees of State Institutions of Higher Learning v. Ray, 172

Board of Trustees of the State of New York v. Fox, 1106, 1235

Board of Trustees of the University of Alabama v. Garrett, 819, 1306, 1310, 1383

Board of Trustees of the University of Arkansas v. Professional Therapy Services, 1364

Board of Trustees of the University of Illinois v. Barrett, 141

Board of Trustees of the University of Illinois v. City of Chicago, 1166

Board of Trustees of the University of Massachusetts & United Automobile, Aerospace & Agricultural Implement Workers of America, 303

Bob Jones University v. Johnson, 1478

Bob Jones University v. United States, 59, 761, 1408n

Boehm v. University of Pennsylvania School of Veterinary Medicine, 728n, 913, 990

Boerne, City of v. Flores, 60, 317, 1298, 1305, 1309

Boettner; People v., 866

Bogart v. Nebraska Student Loan Program, 853

Boise v. Boufford, 521

Boise Junior College District v. Mattefs Construction Co., 1596

Bollard v. California Providence of the Society of Jesus, 944n

Bonnell v. Lorenzo, 635–636, 651, 652–653, 682–683, 745, 1018n

Borough of. See name of borough

Boston Medical Center Corp., 302

Boston University Chapter, AAUP v. NLRB, 494

Bougher v. University of Pittsburgh, 948

Boulahanis v. Board of Regents, 1137, 1140

Boulder, City of v. Regents of the University of Colorado, 1198–1199, 1639

Bourgault v. Yudof, 1212–1213, 1223–1224

Bowen v. American Hospital Association, 1503

Bowers v. NCAA, 1142, 1575, 1578–1581

Bowling v. Scott, 532, 559

Bowling Green, City of v. T. & E. Electrical Contractors, 1162

Boyd; State v., 1086

Boyett v. Troy State University at Montgomery, 530

Boy Scouts of America v. Dale, 1069, 1082, 1430–1431

Braden v. Texas A&M University System, 102

Bradford College & Milk Wagon Drivers & Creamery Workers Union, Local 380, 493

Bradshaw v. Rawlings, 196–197, 208

Brady v. Board of Trustees of Nebraska State Colleges, 472

Brainerd v. Governors of the University of Alberta, 98

Brakeman v. Theta Lambda Chapter of Pi Kappa Alpha, 1096

Brandenburg v. Ohio, 1003, 1052, 1216

Branti v. Finkel, 612

Branzburg v. Hayes, 710

Braxton v. Municipal Court, 1218–1220

Breiner-Sanders v. Georgetown University, 135

Brennan v. King, 105, 135, 139

Brennan v. Stewart, 772

Brentwood Academy v. Tennessee Secondary School Athletic Association, 45n, 49–50, 1546

Bresnick v. Manhattanville College, 538, 540

Bridgeman Art Library, Ltd. v. Corel Corporation, 1353

Bridston v. Dover Corp., 154

Brine v. University of Iowa, 593–594

Broadway Maintenance Corp. v. Rutgers, The State University, 1617

Brockman v. Wyoming Department of Family Services, 317

Brody v. Finch University of Health Sciences/Chicago Medical School, 756–757

Brooklyn Law School v. Aetna Casualty & Surety Co., 152

Brooklyn Law School v. Raybon, Inc., 1601

Brooks v. Auburn University, 1215–1216

Brooks v. Mendoza, 321

Brotherton v. Cleveland, 1290

Brouillette v. Board of Directors of Merged Area IX, 529, 544

Brown v. Armenti, 647–648

Brown v. Board of Education, 758, 1047, 1452

Brown v. Board of Regents of the University of Nebraska, 1213

Brown v. Florida State Board of Regents, 193

Brown v. George Washington University, 37, 481

Brown v. Li, 39, 740–741, 743

Brown v. Trustees of Boston University, 509, 515

Brown v. Wichita State University, 168, 192, 226–227, 242

Brown University; United States v. (5 F.3d 658), 1372

Brown University; United States v. (805 F. Supp. 288), 1371

Brown University; United States v.
  (Civil Action No. 91-CV-3274),
  1371
Brown University & International
  Union, United Automobile,
  Aerospace & Agricultural
  Implement Workers of
  America, 302
Browzin v. Catholic University of
  America, 579–580
Brueckner v. Norwich University,
  748, 1085
Brumbach v. Rensselaer Polytech-
  nic Institute, 572–573
Bruner v. Petersen, 733
Brunner v. New York State Higher
  Education Services Corp., 844
Bruno & Stillman, Inc. v. Globe
  Newspaper Co., 712
Brush v. Pennsylvania State
  University, 1236–1237
Bryant, In re, 845
Bryant v. Independent School Dis-
  trict No. I-38 of Gavin County,
  749
Brzica v. Trustees of Dartmouth
  College, 178, 1082
Brzonkala v. Virginia Polytechnic
  Institute & State University,
  1303
Buchanan v. American Motors
  Corp., 708n
Buchwald v. University of New
  Mexico School of Medicine,
  777–778
Bunger v. University of Oklahoma
  Board of Regents, 676–677,
  679n
Burbridge v. Sampson,
  1005–1006, 1013
Burka v. U.S. Dept. of Health &
  Human Services, 711
Burlington Industries v. Ellerth,
  950
Burnett v. Barnes, 174–175
Burnett v. Grattan, 240–241
Burnham v. Ianni, 692, 995–996,
  999–1001
Burroughs; State v., 866
Burtner v. Hiram College, 953
Burton v. Wilmington Parking
  Authority, 43, 44, 45, 54
Buttny v. Smiley, 1002
Butts v. Higher Education Interim
  Governing Board/Shepherd
  College, 360
Bynes v. Toll, 855, 859
Byrd v. Lamar, 217

C

Cahn v. Antioch University, 179n
Caledonian-Record Publishing Co.
  v. Vermont State College,
  1040, 1280
Califano v. Sanders, 1440

California Cosmetology Coalition v.
  Riley, 1440, 1441, 1442, 1503
California Dental Association v.
  Federal Trade Commission,
  1375
California Faculty Association v.
  Superior Court of Santa Clara
  County, 138–139
California School Employees Asso-
  ciation v. Sunnyvale
  Elementary School District
  of Santa Clara County, 1607
California State Polytechnic
  University-Pomona v.
  Workers' Compensation
  Appeals Board, 321
California State University, Fresno
  v. Gustafson, 847
California State University,
  Hayward v. NCAA, 1572–1573
California Statewide Communities
  Development Authority v. All
  Persons Interested in Matter of
  Validity of Purchase Agree-
  ment, 66
Camara v. Municipal Court, 863
Campanelli v. Bockrath, 364
Campanelli v. Regents of the
  University of California, 219
Canisius College v. City of Buffalo,
  In the Matter of, 1171
Cannon v. University of Chicago,
  127, 128, 1034, 1494–1496
Cantanese v. Ceros-Livingston,
  704
Canterbury Career School, Inc. v.
  Riley, 851
Career Education v. Department of
  Education, 1440, 1487
Carey v. Brown, 1071
Carey v. Piphus, 240, 353
Carlin v. Trustees of Boston
  University, 806
Carlson v. United Academics, 291
Carol "WW" v. Stala, 212
Carpetta v. Pi Kappa Alpha
  Fraternity, 1086
Carr v. St. John's University, New
  York, 727, 924, 988
Cary v. Adams Arapahoe School
  Board, 39n
Catholic Bishop of Chicago; NLRB
  v., 282–286
Cedars of Lebanon Hospital v. Los
  Angeles County, 1184
Central Hudson Gas & Electric
  Corp. v. Public Service
  Commission, 869, 1106, 1233
Central State University v.
  American Association of
  University Professors, 500
Central Wesleyan College v. W. R.
  Grace & Co., 107
Cerrato v. San Francisco Commu-
  nity College District, 238

Certain Scholarship Funds, In re,
  809
Chalenor v. University of North
  Dakota, 1138, 1443
Chan v. Miami University, 546
Chaplinsky v. New Hampshire,
  1023, 1047
Chapman v. Thomas, 1073, 1237
Chapman v. United States, 862
Charles E. Brohawn & Bros., Inc.
  v. Board of Trustees of Chesa-
  peake College, 225–226
Chasin v. Montclair State Univer-
  sity, 154–156, 1276
Chaudhuri v. Tennessee, 72–73
Chavez v. Arte Publico Press, 1351
Chess v. Widmar, 1071
Chevron U.S.A. v. Natural
  Resources Defense Council,
  316, 1442–1443
Chiavarelli v. Williams, 342
Chicago Board of Trade v. United
  States, 1371n
Chicago, City of v. Board of
  Trustees of the University of
  Illinois, 1166
Chicago School of Automatic
  Transmissions v. Accredita-
  tion Alliance of Career
  Schools & Colleges,
  1536–1538, 1542–1543
Chicago Teachers' Union v.
  Hudson, 290, 291n
Childress v. Virginia Common-
  wealth University, 926
Chontos v. Rhea, 952–953, 958
Chou v. University of Chicago &
  Arch Development Corp.,
  1360, 1651
Christensen v. Harris County,
  307–308, 1443
Christophel & Williams v. Univer-
  sity of Cincinnati, 276–277
Chung v. Park, 272–273,
  562, 578
Churchill v. Board of Trustees of
  University of Alabama in
  Birmingham, 1624–1625
Church of the Lukumi Babalu Aye v.
  City of Hialeah, 60–61, 69, 857
Cincinnati, City of v. Discovery
  Network, 1098n
Circuit City Stores, Inc. v. Adams,
  274–275
Citizens Association of
  Georgetown v. District of
  Columbia Board of Zoning
  Adjustment, 1179
Citizens for Alternatives to
  Animal Labs, Inc. v. Board
  of Trustees of the State
  University of New York,
  In re, 1328
City Colleges of Chicago; EEOC v.,
  103
City of. See name of city

City University v. Oregon Office of Educational Policy & Planning, 1268–1269

City University of New York v. Finalco, Inc., 1593–1594

Civil Service Employees Association, Inc., Local 1000, AFSCME v. State University of New York, 277

Claim of. See name of claimant

Clark v. Claremont University Center, 511

Clark v. Community for Creative Non-Violence, 1005, 1006, 1014, 1229

Clark v. Holmes, 628–629, 652

Clark v. Whiting, 502, 552

Clarke v. United States, 1056n

Clarke v. West Virginia Board of Regents, 562–563

Clawson v. Grays Harbor College District No. 2, 484

Clayton v. Trustees of Princeton University, 728n

Cleburne, City of v. Cleburne Living Center, 1181–1182

Clement v. Delgado Community College, 222

Cleveland Board of Education v. Loudermill, 273n, 558, 565

Clinger v. New Mexico Highlands University, Board of Regents, 676–677, 679n, 681

Clissuras v. City University of New York, 238

Coalition for Economic Equity v. Wilson, 791

Coddington v. Adelphi University, 731–732, 1468

Coghlan v. Beta Theta Pi Fraternity, 1091, 1095

Cohen v. Brown University (991 F.2d 888), 123, 1132–1134, 1138

Cohen v. Brown University (101 F.3d 155), 1138

Cohen v. California, 636–637, 1025

Cohen v. San Bernardino Valley College, 636n, 637–641, 649–650

Coker v. Sullivan, 1492

Colangelo v. Theta Psi Chapter of Tau Kappa Epsilon, 1095

Colburn v. Trustees of Indiana University, 669–671

Cole v. Burns International Security Services, 275

Cole v. National Collegiate Athletic Association, 1580

Cole v. Richardson, 612

Coleman v. Gettysburg College, 994

Coleman v. Western Michigan University, 324

College Area Renters & Landlord Association v. City of San Diego, 1182

College Entrance Examination Board v. Pataki, 1355

College Football Association & Capital Cities/ABC, Inc., In re, 1567n

College of Osteopathic Medicine, 497

College of Osteopathic Medicine & Surgery, 494

College Savings Bank v. Florida Prepaid Postsecondary Education Expense Board, 1300–1301, 1310, 1351, 1367

Collins v. Colorado Mountain College, 265

Colorado Association of Public Employees v. Board of Regents of the University of Colorado, 242–243

Colorado Civil Rights Commission v. Regents of the University of Colorado, 1257–1258

Colorado Seminary v. NCAA, 1116

Columbia Union College v. Clarke, 64

Columbia Union College v. Oliver, 64–65

Committee to Save Adelphi v. Daimandopoulos, 1411n

Commonwealth v. See name of opposing party

Communication Workers v. Beck, 290

Community Blood Bank of Kansas City Area v. FTC, 1375

Community College of Allegheny County v. Unemployment Compensation Board of Review, 326

Community College of Delaware County, Appeal of, 1163, 1169

Community College of Philadelphia, 495

Community College System of Nevada v. DR Partners, 1279

Community for Creative Non-Violence v. Reid, 1344

CompuServe, Inc. v. Cyber Promotions, Inc., 867

Conard v. University of Washington, 811, 1125

Conaway v. Smith, 680

Connelly v. University of Vermont, 928

Connick v. Myers, 606, 607–608, 630–631, 647, 1449

Connolly v. County of Orange, 1187–1188

Consolidated Edison Co. v. Public Service Commission, 1236

Consolidated Rail Corp. v. Darrone, 1473–1474, 1496

Constantine v. The Rectors & Visitors of George Mason University, 1307, 1311

Constantino v. University of Pittsburgh, 337

Continental Training Services, Inc. v. Cavazos, 1439, 1443

Cook v. Colgate University, 101–102, 1133n

Cook County Collector v. National College of Education, 1187

Cooper v. Nix, 855, 859

Cooper v. Ross, 696

Cooper, People ex rel. v. Rancho Santiago College, 1163

Cooper Union for Advancement of Science; NLRB v., 493

Cornelius v. NAACP Legal Defense & Education Fund, 997n, 998, 1000, 1075

Cornell University, 281

Cornell University v. Board of Assessors, 1189

Cornforth v. University of Oklahoma Board of Regents, 317

Corporation of Mercer University v. Barrett & Farahany, LLP, 1283

Corporation of Mercer University v. Smith, 178

Corr v. Mattheis, 811

Corry v. Stanford University, 1023, 1047

Corso v. Creighton University, 734

Cort v. Ash, 1494

Cortes v. State of Florida, Board of Regents, 1058

CoStar Group, Inc. v. LoopNet, Inc., 1348

Councill v. Commonwealth, 877

Council of New Jersey State College Locals v. State Board of Higher Education, 595

Coveney v. President & Trustees of the College of the Holy Cross, 735

Cowan v. University of Louisville School of Medicine, 1308

Cowboy Book, Ltd. v. Board of Regents for Agricultural & Mechanical Colleges, 1633

Craft v. Vanderbilt University, 48–49

Craig v. Alabama State University, 511–512

Craig v. Forest Institute of Professional Psychology, 736, 1534n

Craik v. Minnesota State University Board, 124

Craine v. Trinity College, 504–505, 574

Crandell v. New York College of Osteopathic Medicine, 942–943

Crannan v. Maxwell, 1292

Crawford v. Davis, 1464, 1499
Crawford-El v. Britton, 351n
Cremins v. Atlanta Journal, 1283
Crockett v. Edinboro University, 848
Crook v. Baker, 939–941
Cross v. Rector & Visitors of the University of Virginia, 976–977
Crown Cork & Seal Co., 281
Crue v. Aiken, 349, 611, 1120
Cruzan v. Director, Missouri Department of Health, 1289
Curators of University of Missouri v. Brown, 1169, 1249
Cureton v. NCAA, 1574–1577
Curley v. St. John's University, 521
Curran v. Catholic University of America, 486–487, 654, 714
Curtis Publishing Co. v. Butts, 1108n
Cusumano & Yoffie, In re, 711–713
C. W. Post Center of Long Island University, 281

D

Dacosta v. Nwachukwa, 923
Daley v. Wesleyan University, 502, 574
Dallas, City of v. Stanglin, 775
Dallas County Community College District v. Bolton, 173
Dalton; State v., 862
Dambrot v. Central Michigan University, 1018n, 1025, 1120, 1121
Daniel v. American Board of Emergency Medicine, 1374
Dantley v. Howard University, 266–267
Darby v. Bratch, 317
Dartland v. Metropolitan Dade County, 350
Dartmouth Corp. of Alpha Delta v. Town of Hanover, 1195
Dartmouth Review v. Dartmouth College, 989
Davey v. Locke, 69
Davidson v. Board of Governors of State Colleges & Universities, 518
Davidson v. University of North Carolina at Chapel Hill, 1149
Davidson & Jones, Inc. v. North Carolina Department of Administration, 1617–1618
Davis v. Goode, 938
Davis v. Goord, 610
Davis v. Halpern, 788
Davis v. J. F. Drake State Technical College, 276
Davis v. Monroe County Board of Education, 749, 750–752, 1464, 1487, 1497n

Davis v. Oregon State University, 553–554
Davis v. Southerland, 356
Davis v. Williams, 532n
Dean v. Wissman, 341
DeBauche v. Trani, 53–54, 1216
DeCanas v. Bica, 780
Decker v. Oklahoma State Technical University, 324–325
Defoor v. Evesque, 334
DeFunis v. Odegaard, 784–785, 797–799
Dehaan v. Brandeis University, 924
Deitchman v. E. R. Squibb & Sons, Inc., 708–709
De La Cruz v. Tormey, 899–900
Delaware State College v. Ricks, 103
Delbridge v. Maricopa County Community College District, 203
Delgado v. Stegall, 951, 952, 1464
de Llano v. Berglund, 564–565, 678–681, 697
Del Papa v. Board of Regents of University & Community College System of Nevada, 1277
Delta Tau Delta v. Johnson, 1093
DePaul University v. Rosewell, 1637
Deras v. Myers, 124–125
Derdeyn v. University of Colorado, 1143
DeRonde v. Regents of the University of California, 788
DeShaney v. Winnebago County Department of Social Services, 353–354, 357
Desyllas v. Bernstine, 1014
Determination of Executive Commission on Ethical Standards, In re, 1242, 1274
Detroit College of Business & Detroit College of Business Faculty Association, 495
Devers v. Southern University, 864–865
Diamond v. Chakrabarty, 1356–1357
Diamond v. Diehr, 1357
DiBona v. Matthews, 637, 644
Dickson; People v., 1207–1208
Dickson v. Sitterson, 1215
DiLoreto v. Downey Unified School District Board of Education, 1014n
Dilworth v. Dallas Community College District, 937
Dinnan, In re, 700–701
Dinnan v. Regents of the University System of Georgia, 125–126

Dinu v. Harvard College, 938
Disesa v. St. Louis Community College, 937
Dismissal Proceedings Against Huang, 564
Dismuke v. Quaynor, 212–213
District of Columbia v. Catholic Education Press, 1193
Dixon v. Alabama State Board of Education, 725, 974
Doe v. See name of opposing party
Doherty v. Southern College of Optometry, 731, 772
Dolan v. City of Tigard, 1170
Dole v. Shenandoah Baptist Church, 308
Donahue v. State, 1278
Donnelley v. Rhode Island Board of Governors for Higher Education, 519
Donohue v. Copiague Unified Free School District, 214
Doria v. University of Vermont, 191–192
Dorsett v. Board of Trustees for State Colleges & Universities, 529, 668–669
Doru Tsaganea, In re Claim of, 326
Dow Chemical Co. v. Allen, 707–708
Draughon Training Institute, In re, 1554
Drogaris v. Trustees of Columbia University, 202–203
DTH Publishing Corp. v. The University of North Carolina at Chapel Hill, 1040
Duarte v. Commonwealth, 866
Dube v. State University of New York, 637
Dubilier; United States v., 1651
Duck Inn, Inc. v. Montana State University-Northern, 1630–1631
Duello v. Board of Regents, University of Wisconsin, 510, 1474
Duffield v. Robertson Stephens & Company, 274
Duffy; United States v., 1436
Dugan v. Stockton State College, 545
Dugan & Meyers Construction Co. v. State of Ohio Department of Administrative Services, 1615–1616
Duke v. The American University, 1180n
Dunkel v. Elkins, 1220–1221
Duquesne University of the Holy Ghost & Duquesne University Law School Faculty Association, 494
Dybczak v. Tuskegee Institute, 513

Dynamic Student Services v. State System of Higher Education, 1284

E

Easley v. Cromartie, 1205
Easley v. University of Michigan Board of Regents, 981
Eastern Connecticut State University v. Connecticut Freedom of Information Commission, 1036
Eastern Railroad Presidents Conference v. Noerr Motor Freight, 1370, 1546
Eastman v. University of Michigan, 827–828, 829–830
Eden v. Board of Trustees of State University, 579n, 727, 756
Educational Credit Management Corp. v. Ross, 845
Edwards v. Aguillard, 621
Edwards v. California University of Pennsylvania, 39, 625, 634, 647, 648
Edwards v. Wallace Community College, 351
EEOC v. See name of opposing party
E. I. DuPont de Nemours & Co. v. Okuley, 1360, 1651
Eiland v. Wolf, 731, 733–734
Eiseman v. State, 882
El-Attar v. Mississippi State University, 767
Elcom, Ltd.; United States v., 1354
Eldred v. Ashcroft, 128, 1354
Electromation v. NLRB, 281
Eli Lilly & Co. v. Sav-On Drugs, 1268n
Elkins v. Moreno, 827, 835
El Kouni v. Trustees of Boston University, 926
Elliott v. City of Athens, 1182–1183
Ellison v. Robertson, 1348
Elmira College, 494
Elsinore Christian Center v. City of Lake Elsinore, 60n
Elter v. Great Lakes Higher Education Corp., 846
Emery v. Boise State University & Embry Riddle Aeronautical, 326
Emory University v. Porubiansky, 158
Employees of Temple University, In the Matter of, 301–302
Employment Division v. Smith, 59–60, 744, 890n, 891n, 1266n
Encore College Bookstores, Inc. v. Auxiliary Services Corp. of

State University of New York at Farmingdale, 248
Engel v. Vitale, 57
Enright v. California State University, 525n
Epilepsy Foundation of Northeast Ohio v. NLRB, 279
Epperson v. Arkansas, 621
Equal Access Education v. Merton (305 F. Supp. 585), 779–781
Equal Access Education v. Merton (325 F. Supp. 655), 781
Erzinger v. Regents of the University of California, 890
Escobar v. State University of New York/College at Old Westbury, 169–170
Estate of. See name of decedent
Esteban v. Central Missouri State College, 168, 915, 922, 975–976, 978
Evans v. Employment Security Department, 326
Evans v. Newton, 49–50
Evans v. West Virginia Board of Regents, 804–805
Excelsior College v. New York State Education Department, In the Matter of, 1261
Ex parte. See name of party
Ezrailson v. Rohrich, 340

F

Fabunmi v. University of Maryland at College Park, 505–506
Faculty of City University of New York Law School at Queens College v. Murphy, 184
Fairleigh Dickinson University & Fairleigh Dickinson University Council of American Association of University Professors Chapters, 494
Faragher v. City of Boca Raton, 950
Farmington v. Tokushige, 41
Farnsworth v. The Proctor & Gamble Co., 708
Faro v. New York University, 502
Fauley v. Forrest County, Mississippi, 1205n
Faulkner v. Jones, 767
Faur v. Jewish Theological Seminary of America, 271–272
Favia v. Indiana University of Pennsylvania, 1134n
Fay v. Thiel College, 156–157, 158
Fayetteville, City of v. Phillips, 1191–1192
F. Buddie Contracting, Ltd. v. Cuyahoga Community College District, 352, 1615
FDIC v. Providence College, 183–184

Federal Maritime Commission v. South Carolina Ports Authority, 1298, 1304, 1311
Federated Publications v. Board of Trustees of Michigan State University, 1279
Felder v. Casey, 239
Feldman v. Ho, 130, 625, 677–678, 680–681
Feldman v. Regents of the University of New Mexico, 173
Fellheimer v. Middlebury College, 729, 990
Felton v. Recording Industry Association of America, 1354
Ferguson v. Greater Pocatello Chamber of Commerce, 1633
Ferrer v. Trustees of the University of Pennsylvania, 475
Fieno v. State of Minnesota, 339
Finley v. National Endowment for the Arts, 648
Finstand v. Washburn University of Topeka, 214
First Equity Corp. of Florida v. Utah State University, 172–173, 227n
Fisher v. Dillard University, 512
Fisher v. Vassar College, 503–504, 526
Fitzpatrick v. Bitzer, 1304, 1309
Flanagan v. President & Directors of Georgetown College, 820–821, 1471
Fleming v. New York University, 858
Flores v. Morgan Hill Unified School District, 959
Florida Board of Regents v. Armesto, 103–104, 133
Florida ex rel. Hawkins v. Board of Control, 758, 1452
Florida Memorial College; NLRB v., 493
Florida Prepaid Postsecondary Education Expense Board v. College Savings Bank, 1310, 1360–1361
Florida State University v. Dann, 1286
Foley Brothers v. Filardo, 1484
Fong v. Purdue University, 563–564
Forasté v. Brown University, 1344–1345
Forbes v. Napolitano, 1290
Forbes v. Woods, 1289–1290
Ford v. Nicks, 509
Ford v. Schering-Plough, 1578
Fordice; United States v., 758–759, 1456–1460
Forester v. State of New York, 222
Forsham v. Harris, 1506n
Forsyth County v. Nationalist Movement, 1010n

44 Liquormart v. Rhode Island, 1106, 1236

Forum for Academic & Institutional Rights (FAIR), Inc. v. Rumsfeld, 1429–1432

Foster v. Board of Trustees of Butler County Community College, 197–198, 748

Foster v. Purdue University, 1089

Foundation for Interior Design Education Research v. Savannah College of Art & Design, 1542, 1549

Fox v. Board of Supervisors of Louisiana State University & Agricultural & Mechanical College, 1150

Fox v. Board of Trustees of State University of New York, 1235n

Frabotta v. Meridia Huron Hospital School, 930

Frank v. Ivy Club, 1068

Frank Briscoe Co. v. Rutgers, the State University, 142

Franklin v. Gwinnett County Public Schools, 121, 749, 946–947, 1463, 1467, 1496–1498

Franklin & Marshall College; EEOC v., 701

Franklin & Marshall College v. Zoning Hearing Board of the City of Lancaster, 1172

Fraser v. Nationwide Mutual Insurance Co., 1385

Freeman v. Busch, 210

Friday v. Uzzell, 1066–1067

Frisby v. Schultz, 1028

Frumkin v. Board of Trustees, Kent State, 560

Fruth v. New York University, 773

Fry v. Board of Regents of University of Wisconsin System, 1060

Fry v. United States, 1301

Fu v. University of Nebraska, 202

Fuller v. Rayburn, 1499

Funk Brothers Seed Co. v. Kalo Inoculant Co., 1356

Furek v. University of Delaware, 208–209, 1084, 1087

Furomoto v. Lyman, 1016–1017

Furutani v. Ewigleben, 918

Futrell v. Ahrens, 855–856

Futrelle v. Duke University, 138

G

Gabrilowitz v. Newman, 920, 979

Gade v. National Solid Waste Management Association, 305

Gaffney v. Cummings, 1205

Gaines v. NCAA, 1569–1570

Gaither v. Wake Forest University, 361–362

Galdikas v. Fagan, 1534n

Galiatsatos v. University of Akron, 574

Galloway v. Roger Williams University, 266

Gally v. Columbia University, 229

Gamma Phi Chapter of Sigma Chi Building Fund Corp. v. Dade County, 1191

Gamma Phi Chapter of Sigma Chi Fraternity v. University of Miami, 1081

Ganden v. NCAA, 1142, 1577–1581

Gannett Rivers States Publishing Corp. v. Mississippi State University, 1035–1036

Garcia v. San Antonio Metropolitan Transit Authority, 1302

Garcia v. S.U.N.Y. Health Sciences Center of Brooklyn, 807

Gardetto v. Mason (Eastern Wyoming College), 679n

Gardiner v. Tschechtelin, 477

Garner v. Michigan State University, 566

Garofalo v. Lambda Chi Alpha, 1096

Garrett v. Matthews, 532, 807

Garrett v. University of Alabama at Birmingham Board of Trustees, 1312, 1500

Garrison v. Louisiana, 219, 1109

Garstang v. Superior Court of Los Angeles County, 136n

Garvie v. Jackson, 569

Gaskill v. Ft. Hays State University, 578, 1287

Gaspar v. Bruton, 928–929, 982–983

Gay Activists Alliance v. Board of Regents of University of Oklahoma, 1053

Gay & Lesbian Students Association v. Gohn, 1053–1054, 1102

Gay Law Students v. Board of Trustees, 1432

Gay Lesbian Bisexual Alliance v. Pryor, 1054–1055

Gay Lesbian Bisexual Alliance v. Sessions, 1054

Gay Lib v. University of Missouri, 1053

Gay Men's Health Crisis v. Sullivan, 1442, 1446

Gay Rights Coalition of Georgetown University Law Center v. Georgetown University, 1055–1056

Gay Student Services v. Texas A&M University, 1051n

Gay Students Organization of the University of New Hampshire v. Bonner, 1051–1052

Gebser v. Lago Vista Independent School District, 750–752, 948–950, 953, 1136, 1487, 1497n

Gedes v. Northwest Missouri State University, 472

Gehling v. St. George's School of Medicine, 99, 197

Geier v. Alexander, 796, 1454n

Geier v. Sundquist, 125, 1454n

Geier v. University of Tennessee, 1453–1454

General Dynamics Corp. v. Superior Court, 141n

General Telephone Company of the Northwest v. EEOC, 106n

George v. University of Idaho, 958

George Washington University v. District of Columbia, 1175

George Washington University v. District of Columbia Board of Zoning Adjustment, 1175

Georgia Association of Educators v. Harris, 268

Gernander v. Winona State University, 338

Gertz v. Robert Welch, Inc., 219, 1108n, 1551

Gibbs Construction Co. v. Board of Supervisors of Louisiana State University, 1613

Giebel v. Sylvester, 612, 1013, 1014, 1223

Gilbert v. Homar, 569–570

Gilbert v. Seton Hall University, 194

Giles v. Howard University, 804

Gill v. Franklin Pierce Law Center, 806, 963

Gilmer v. Interstate-Johnson Lane, 137, 274, 299

Girardier v. Webster College, 846, 848

Givhan v. Western Line Consolidated School District, 606–607, 608, 672

Gladney v. Thomas, 509n

Glassboro, Borough of v. Vallorosi, 1181

Glenbrook Road Association v. District of Columbia Board of Zoning Adjustment, 1179–1180

Glockson; United States v., 850

Glover v. Cole, 1237–1238

Goehring v. Brophy, 890–891

Goldberg v. Northeastern University, 194

Goldberg v. Regents of the University of California, 168–169

Goldfarb v. Virginia State Bar, 1369, 1547

Gomes v. University of Maine System, 980–981

Gomez v. Toledo, 348

Gomez-Gil v. University of Hartford, 321

Gomillion v. Lightfoot, 782

Gonzaga University v. Doe, 1033, 1437, 1487
Gonzaga University; Doe v., 48n, 212, 219–220, 1034
Gonzales v. National Board of Medical Examiners, 961–962
Gonzales v. Raich, 1303
Gonzalez v. North American College of Louisiana, 817
Good v. Associated Students of the University of Washington, 1057
Goodisman v. Lytle, 553
Goodkind v. University of Minnesota, 473
Goodman v. President & Trustees of Bowdoin College, 731
Goodman & Barnard College, In re, 326–327
Goodman, People ex rel. v. University of Illinois Foundation, 1192
Good News Club v. Milford Central School, 58n, 998, 1238n
Goodreau v. Rector & Visitors of the University of Virginia, 941
Goodwin v. Keuka College, 962–963
Gorenberg v. Onondaga County Board of Elections, 1200
Gorman v. St. Raphael Academy, 55
Gorman v. University of Rhode Island, 979
Goss v. Lopez, 939–940, 975, 980, 984
Goss v. San Jacinto Junior College, 237, 694–695
Gossett v. State of Oklahoma ex rel. Board of Regents, 805–806
Gott v. Berea College, 10
Gottschalk v. Benson, 1357
Graczyk v. Workers' Compensation Appeals Board, 324
Graduate Employees Organization v. Illinois Educational Labor Relations Board, 302
Gragg v. Wichita State University, 200
Grand Jury Subpoena, In re, 710–711
Grandson v. University of Minnesota, 1136–1137
Grant v. Tulane University, 321
Gratz v. Bollinger, 523, 791–803, 821–823, 825
Gray v. Board of Higher Education, 132, 701
Gray v. Board of Regents of University System of Georgia, 545
Gray v. Mundelein College, 482, 585–586
Grayned v. City of Rockford, 1003, 1007

Great A&P Tea Co. v. Cottrell, 1268
Greaton Properties v. Lower Merion Township, 1180
Green v. County School Board, 1454
Green v. Trinity International University, 224
Greenberg v. CBS, Inc., 1113
Greene v. Howard University, 480, 1582
Greenhill v. Bailey, 983
Greenya v. George Washington University, 44, 46n
Gregorich v. Lund, 349
Gregory v. Hunt, 361
Grider v. Cavazos, 852
Grimes v. Kennedy Krieger Institute, Inc., 1291, 1648–1650
Grine v. Board of Trustees, University of Arkansas, 100
Griswold v. Connecticut, 618–619, 652
Grody v. State, 1220
Gross v. Family Services Agency & Nova Southeastern University, Inc., 203–204
Grossner v. Trustees of Columbia University, 918
Grove v. Ohio State University, 754–755
Grove City College v. Bell, 1128–1129, 1478, 1479–1480, 1573
Grutter v. Bollinger, 128–129, 523, 527–528, 619n, 626–627, 788, 791–803, 821–823, 825
Guardians Association v. Civil Service Commission of the City of New York, 1451, 1474–1477, 1495
Guckenberger v. Boston University (957 F. Supp. 306), 963–964
Guckenberger v. Boston University (974 F. Supp. 106), 964–965, 966–967
Guckenberger v. Boston University (8 F. Supp. 2d 82), 967–968
Guidi v. California, 1165
Gulf Regional Education Television Affiliates v. University of Houston, 243
Guste, State ex rel. v. Nicholls College Foundation, 247–248, 1281
Gutzwiller v. University of Cincinnati, 508–509

H

Haben v. Anderson, 1090n
Hack v. President & Fellows of Yale College, 857–858, 1371

Hackel v. Vermont State Colleges, 500
Hadley v. Junior College District, 1205
Hadley v. North Arkansas Community Technical College, 237–238
Hafer v. Melo, 231n, 347
Haffer v. Temple University, 1131–1132, 1479
Hahn v. Vermont Law School, 98–99
Hairston v. Pacific 10 Conference, 1570, 1572
Halasz v. University of New England, 966
Hall v. Kutztown University, 682n
Hall v. Medical College of Ohio at Toledo, 235–236
Hall v. University of Minnesota, 1116
Hall v. Virginia, 877
Hallal v. RDV Sports, Inc., 322
Halper; United States v., 919
Hamilton v. Regents of the University of California, 10
Hamilton Chapter of Alpha Delta Phi v. Hamilton College, 1082, 1371
Hammarstrom, In re, 845
Hammond v. Brown, 623
Hammond v. South Carolina State College, 1008–1009
Hand v. Mitchell, 941
Hander v. San Jacinto Junior College, 237, 686–687
H & V Engineering, Inc. v. Board of Professional Engineers and Land Surveyors, 532n
Hans v. Louisiana, 1308
Hanson v. Kynast, 1149, 1151
Harden v. Adams, 696
Hardin v. Phillips, 334
Hardy v. Jefferson Community College, 642–644, 651, 653, 742n
Harlow v. Fitzgerald, 348
Harper v. Board of Regents, Illinois State University, 1140
Harrell v. Southern Illinois University, 1204
Harrington v. Harris, 521, 530, 609–610
Harris v. Blake, 985–986
Hartford Accident & Indemnity Co. v. Village of Hempstead, 157
Hartman v. Merged Area VI Community College, 594–595
Hartwig v. Albertus Magnus College, 490
Harvard Manual on Tax Aspects of Charitable Giving, 1415n
Harwood v. Johns Hopkins University, 732–733, 938
Hatchett v. Philander Smith College, 316

Hawes v. Emory University, 809

Hawkins v. NCAA, 1116

Hayden v. University of Notre Dame, 200–201, 1212n

Hays County Guardian v. Supple, 1098, 1238–1239

Hayut v. State University of New York, 52n, 745n, 748, 943, 944, 951, 956–957

Hazelwood School District v. Kuhlmeier, 39, 632, 642, 650, 740, 743, 1102–1103

Healy v. James, 629, 738, 995–996, 1003, 1004, 1009–1010, 1051–1052, 1071, 1101, 1107, 1210, 1227

Healy v. Larsson, 727

HEB Ministries, Inc. v. Texas Higher Education Coordinating Board, 1266–1267

Heffron v. International Society for Krishna Consciousness, 1013n, 1073, 1229

Heinritz v. Lawrence University, 266

Heirs & Wrongful Death Beneficiaries of Branning v. Hinds Community College District, 1620–1621

Helvering v. Davis, 1299

Henderson State University v. Spadoni, 974

Hendricks v. Clemson University, 215–216, 1127

Hendrickson v. Amazon.com, Inc., 1349

Hendrickson v. eBay, Inc., 1348, 1349

Hennessey v. Coastal Eagle Point Oil Company, 269

Hensley v. Erie Insurance Co., 158

Henson v. Honor Committee of the University of Virginia, 976

Herbert v. Lando, 1109

Hernandez, Estate of v. Board of Regents, 1088–1089

Hernandez-Wheeler v. Flavio, 1089

Herzog Foundation v. University of Bridgeport, 181

Hess v. Port Authority Trans-Hudson Corp., 238

Hetrick v. Martin, 628

Hewitt v. Helms, 555

Hibbs v. Department of Human Resources, 316

Hickey v. Zezulka, 879

Hickman v. Taylor, 110

Higher Education Coordinating Council/Roxbury Community College v. Massachusetts Teachers' Association, 499

Hildebrand v. Board of Trustees of Michigan State University, 94–95, 696

Hill v. Board of Trustees of Michigan State University, 980

Hill v. Colorado, 636

Hill v. NCAA, 1145–1146, 1564

Hill v. Ross, 524–525

Hill v. Talladega College, 544–545

Hillis v. Stephen F. Austin State University, 696

Hillsborough County v. Automated Medical Laboratories, 1297n

Hollister v. Tuttle, 569

Holm v. Ithaca College, 531

Honadle v. University of Vermont & State Agricultural College, 234n

Hoover v. Morales, 1242–1243

Hopf v. Topcorp, Inc., 1278–1279, 1281

Hopwood v. Texas, 788–790, 800–801

Horowitz v. Board of Curators of the University of Missouri, 983–985, 987

Horton v. Commonwealth of Pennsylvania, 877

Hoshijo ex rel. White; State v., 1028, 1121n

Hosty v. Carter, 39, 1097n, 1105

House Bill 2620, In re, 1205–1206

Howard Savings Institution v. Peep, 810

Howard University v. Best, 37, 573

Howard University v. Good Food Services, Inc., 1595

Howlett v. Rose, 239

Howren, In re, 847n

H. P. Hood & Sons v. DuMond, 1269

Huang v. Board of Governors of the University of North Carolina, 568

Huddleston v. University of Vermont, 831

Hudson v. Craven, 644

Hudson v. United States, 919–920

Hudson v. Wesley College, 541

Hughes v. Beta Upsilon Building Association, 1089

Hulen v. Yates, 568–569, 679–681

Hull v. Cuyahoga Valley Joint Vocational School District Board of Education, 351

Humana of Illinois, Inc. v. Board of Trustees of Southern Illinois University, 1633

Hunt v. McNair, 62–63

Hunt v. State of Missouri, Department of Corrections, 258n

Hunt v. University of Alaska at Fairbanks, 755n

Hunter; State v., 863, 864

Hupart v. Board of Higher Education of the City of New York, 797

Hupp v. Sasser, 340–341

Hutto v. Finney, 123

Hyman v. International Business Machines Corp., 342

Hynes v. Mayor & Council of Oradell, 1007

I

IBP, Inc. v. Alvarez, 311

Idaho v. Coeur d' Alene Tribe of Idaho, 1311n

IIT Research Institute v. United States, 1653

Illini Media Company v. Department of Revenue, 1193–1194

Illinois Nurses Association v. Board of Trustees of the University of Illinois, 140

Imperiale v. Hahnemann University, 47, 940

Indiana ex rel. Anderson v. Brand, 272, 479

In re. See name of party

Inspector of Buildings of Salem v. Salem State College, 1165–1166

Institute of Computer Technology; United States v., 1436

Inter-Faculty Organization v. Carlson, 1247

International Association of Machinists v. Street, 290

International Ladies Garment Workers Union v. NLRB, 288

International Primate Protection League v. Institute for Behavioral Research, Inc., 1327

International Society for Krishna Consciousness v. Lee, 998n, 999

International Textbook Co. v. Pigg, 1268

In the Matter of. See name of party

Iota Xi Chapter of Sigma Chi Fraternity v. George Mason University, 1022–1023, 1086

Iowa Hotel Association v. State Board of Regents, 1624

Iowa State University of Science & Technology v. United States, 1634, 1636

Iron Arrow Honor Society v. Heckler, 1479

Ithaca College & Ithaca College Faculty Association, 494

Ivy Club v. Edwards, 100, 1068n

J

Jaar v. University of Miami, 242, 1292

Jackson v. Birmingham Board of Education, 1483–1484

Jackson v. Culinary School of Washington, 853, 1376

Jackson v. Drake University, 1127
Jackson v. Metropolitan Edison
  Co., 44, 45
Jackson v. Strayer College, 1050,
  1055
Jacobs v. Mundelein College, 482
Jaffee v. Redmond, 112–113
Jain v. State of Iowa, 210–211
Jaksa v. Regents of the University
  of Michigan, 981
James v. Langford, 1253
James v. Nelson, 1203–1204
James, State ex rel. v. Ohio State
  University, 704–705, 1285
Janes v. Jane, 335–336
Jansen v. Atiyeh, 1625–1627
Jarzynka v. St. Thomas University
  School of Law, 925
Javetz v. Board of Control, Grand
  Valley State University, 513
Jefferson County Pharmaceutical
  Association v. Abbott Labora-
  tories, 1370, 1600, 1632
Jeffries v. Harleston, 609, 656n,
  684, 689–691, 1018n
Jeldness v. Pearce, 783
Jenkins v. Louisiana State Board
  of Education, 922, 978, 1007
Jesik v. Maricopa County Commu-
  nity College District, 883–884
Jew v. University of Iowa, 510
J. I. Case Co. v. NLRB, 289
Jiminez v. Almodovar, 582,
  584–585
Jirau-Bernal v. Agrait, 612
John Grace & Co. v. State Univer-
  sity Construction Fund, 1617
Johns Hopkins University v. Ritter,
  184, 472, 546–547
Johnson v. Board of Regents of
  University of Georgia, 789n
Johnson v. Board of Regents of
  University of Wisconsin
  System, 588–590
Johnson v. Christian Brothers
  College, 545
Johnson v. Colorado State Board
  of Agriculture, 543
Johnson v. Dallas Independent
  School District, 355, 356
Johnson v. Edinboro State College,
  847–848
Johnson v. Lincoln University,
  672–674, 677
Johnson v. Louisiana Department
  of Education, 818–819
Johnson v. Schmitz, 216,
  732, 735
Johnson v. Southern Greek
  Housing Corp., 1189
Johnson v. Southern University,
  1287–1288
Johnson v. Transportation
  Agency, 800
Johnson v. University System of
  Georgia, 782n, 783

Johnson-Taylor v. Gannon,
  590–591
Jolicoeur v. Mihaly, 1199–1200
Jones v. Alfred H. Mayer Co.,
  1305
Jones v. Board of Governors, 913
Jones v. Board of Regents of the
  University System of Georgia,
  330
Jones v. Illinois Department of
  Rehabilitation Services, 894
Jones v. Kappa Alpha Order,
  1092, 1094
Jones v. Tennessee State Board of
  Education, 978, 979
Jones v. University of Central
  Oklahoma, 470
Jones v. University of North
  Carolina, 122
Jones v. University of Pennsylva-
  nia, 362–363
Jones v. Wittenberg University,
  878
Jones v. Wolf, 59n
Joye v. Hunterdon Central
  Regional High School Board of
  Education, 1146
Joyner v. Whiting, 1065–1066,
  1100–1101
Judson v. Essex Agricultural &
  Technical Institute, 322–323
Jung v. Association of American
  Medical Colleges (300 F. Supp.
  2d 119), 1373
Jung v. Association of American
  Medical Colleges (339 F. Supp.
  2d 26), 1373
Junger v. Daly, 1394
J. Weingarten, Inc.; NLRB v., 279

K

Kadiki v. Virginia Commonwealth
  University, 943, 953
Kaiser Aetna v. United States, 55
Kaltenberger v. Ohio College of
  Podiatric Medicine, 968–969
Kamehameha Schools/Bernice
  Pauahi Bishop Estate; Doe v.,
  761, 783n, 821n
Kanaly v. State of South Dakota,
  1252
Kania v. Fordham, 1098
Kantor v. Schmidt, 935n
Kappa Alpha Educational Founda-
  tion, Inc. v. Holliday, 1190
Kaprelian v. Texas Woman's
  University, 550
Karibian v. Columbia University,
  944
Karle v. Board of Trustees/
  Marshall University, 573
Karr v. Board of Trustees of Michi-
  gan State University, 271
Kashani v. Purdue University,
  234–235

Kashif v. Central State University,
  480
Kaspar Wire Works, Inc. v.
  Secretary of Labor, 304
Katz v. Georgetown University,
  480
Katz v. United States, 1207
Katzenbach v. Morgan, 1304
Kavanagh v. Trustees of Boston
  University, 1152
Kay v. Board of Higher Education,
  623
Kazmier v. Widmann, 316
K.D. v. Educational Testing
  Service, 734
Keams v. Tempe Technical Insti-
  tute (39 F.3d 222),
  853, 1553
Keams v. Tempe Technical Insti-
  tute (110 F.3d 44), 1553
Keddie v. Rutgers, The State
  University, 1285
Kedroff v. Saint Nicholas
  Cathedral, 59n
Keegan v. University of Delaware,
  58n
Keen v. Penson, 646
Keles v. Yale University, 757
Keller v. State Bar of California,
  1059
Kelley v. Board of Trustees of Uni-
  versity of Illinois, 1137, 1138
Kelly v. Arriba Soft Corporation,
  1340
Kelly v. Gwinnell, 210
Kelly v. Yale University, 745n,
  749
Kelm v. Carlson, 827
Kendall Memorial School v. NLRB,
  493
Kenner v. Kappa Alpha Psi Frater-
  nity, 1094–1095
Kern v. University of Notre Dame
  du Lac, 703
Keyishian v. Board of Regents,
  611, 619–621, 650, 738, 1270
Khademi v. South Orange Commu-
  nity College District,
  1001–1002, 1005–1006, 1009,
  1013, 1106
Kientzy v. McDonnell Douglass
  Corp., 136n
Kilcoyne v. Morgan, 555–556
Kimel v. Florida Board of
  Regents, 1305–1307, 1309,
  1310
Kincaid v. Gibson, 39, 1097,
  1102–1105
Kinder v. Industrial Claim Appeals
  Office of the State of Colorado,
  322
King v. Board of Control of East-
  ern Michigan University,
  1485–1486
King v. Riverside Regional Medical
  Center, 96

King v. University of Minnesota, 536, 559–560

Kingery Construction Co. v. Board of Regents of the University of Nebraska, 1612

Kirsch v. Prince Georges County, 1181

Kirschenbaum v. Northwestern University, 471–472

Kirwan v. Diamondback, 1039

Kissinger v. Reporters Committee for Freedom of the Press, 1506n

Klan-Rastani v. Clark University, 321

Klein v. Solomon, 335

Kleindienst v. Mandel, 1317

Klein Independent School District v. Mattox, 1030n

Kleinknecht v. Gettysburg College, 207–208, 1148–1150

Klemencic v. Ohio State University, 953

Knapp v. Northwestern University, 1141

Kneeland v. NCAA, 1565

Kniepp v. Tedder, 354

Knight v. Alabama, 1461

Knight v. Minnesota Community College Faculty Association, 287, 498

Knoll v. Board of Regents of the University of Nebraska, 209, 861, 882, 1092

Knowles v. Ohio State University, 264

Kobluk v. University of Minnesota, 110

Kobrin v. University of Minnesota, 537

Korf v. Ball State University, 532–533

Kort v. Diversified Collection Services, 848

Kovats v. Rutgers, The State University, 234n, 235

Kracunas & Pallett v. Iona College, 943, 947

Kraft v. William Alanson White Psychiatric Foundation, 338

Krasnow v. Virginia Polytechnic Institute, 913, 915

Krause v. Rhodes, 347n

Krebs v. Rutgers, The State University of New Jersey, 1034n

Kroll v. Board of Trustees of the University of Illinois, 193

Krotkoff v. Goucher College, 37, 582–584

Krynicky v. University of Pittsburgh, 47, 50n

Ku v. State of Tennessee, 987n

Kumbhojkar v. University of Miami, 540–541

Kunda v. Muhlenberg College, 127, 131–132, 506–508, 515

Kunz v. New York, 1010n

Kurtz v. Vickrey, 672

Kwiatkowski v. Ithaca College, 988

Kyriakopoulos v. George Washington University, 130

Kyriazis v. West Virginia University, 156, 159, 734

L

Lafayette College v. Commissioner, Department of Labor & Industry, 704

Lafayette College v. Zoning Hearing Board of the City of Easton, 1174

Laidlow v. Hariton Machinery Co., 320

Laird v. Tatum, 1211

Lake County Estates v. Tahoe Regional Planning Agency, 232, 1308

Lake of the Ozarks Community College Steering Committee, State ex rel. v. Coordinating Board for Higher Education, 1252

Lam v. Curators of University of Missouri, 1481–1482

Lamb's Chapel v. Center Moriches Union Free School District, 58n, 1000, 1075, 1212, 1238n

Lamphere v. Brown University, 106, 514

Lanvermeyer v. Denison University, 532

Lance; Doe v., 1464

Lane v. Pena, 1468

Lanford, In re, 847

Lansdale v. Tyler Junior College, 38

Lapides v. Board of Regents of the University System of Georgia, 97, 1308

LaPorte, Application of, 1172

Larson v. Board of Regents of the University of Nebraska, 1098

Lau v. Nichols, 1475

Laura O. v. State, 884–885

Lavin-McEleney v. Marist College, 520

Law v. National Collegiate Athletic Association, 1567–1568

Lawhorne v. Harlan, 336

Lawrence v. Curators of the University of Missouri, 537

Lawrence v. Texas, 688

Lawrence Bicentennial Commission v. Appleton, Wisconsin, 1240

Leach v. New Mexico Junior College, 237

League of United Latin American Citizens; United States v., 759–760

League of United Latin American Citizens v. Wilson (908 F. Supp. 755), 839–840

League of United Latin American Citizens v. Wilson (997 F. Supp. 1244), 840

League of United Latin American Citizens v. Wilson (1998 WL 141325), 840

Leathers v. Medlock, 1448

Lebron v. National Railroad Passenger Corp., 51, 248–249, 858

Lee v. International Society for Krishna Consciousness, 1013n

Lee v. Life Insurance Co. of North America, 892–893

Lee v. Paige, 852

Lee v. Trustees of Dartmouth College, 962, 1468

Lee v. Weisman, 58, 72, 73

Leeds v. Meltz, 51, 1102

Leffall v. Dallas Independent School District, 355

Legal Services Corporation v. Velazquez, 901

Lehnert v. Ferris Faculty Association, 290–291, 1059

Lekutis v. University of Osteopathic Medicine, 993

Lemon v. Kurtzman, 62, 1070–1071

Lemoyne-Owens College, 493

Leonard; People v., 1218

Lesage v. State of Texas, 790n, 1499

Lesage v. University of Texas, 1311

Lesser v. Board of Education of New York, 754

Leticia A. v. Regents of the University of California, 838–839

Levin v. Harleston, 655–658, 740n

Levin v. Yeshiva University, 860–861

Levine v. George Washington University, 755, 803–804

Levitt v. University of Texas, 558

Levy v. Scranton, 1201

Levy v. University of Cincinnati, 272

Lewis v. Loyola University of Chicago, 473–474, 474

Lewis v. St. Cloud State University, 191, 1113

Lewis v. Salem Academy & College, 37, 482

Lewis v. Wilson, 1003

Lewis & Clark College, 494

Lewis University, 284

Lewis University; NLRB v., 494

Lexington-Fayette Urban County Board of Health v. Board of Trustees of the University of Kentucky, 1162–1163

Lexington Theological Seminary v. Vance, 931–932

L'ggrke v. Benkula, 816, 1437

Lidecker v. Kendall College, 1534n

Lieber v. Board of Trustees of Southern Illinois University, 1284

Lieberman v. University of Chicago, 1496

Lifchez v. Hartigan, 1289

Lim v. Trustees of Indiana University, 538

Lincoln v. Board of Regents of the University System of Georgia, 512

Lincoln County v. Luning, 1308

Linden Lumber Division v. NLRB, 288

Lingle v. Norge Division of Magic Chef, 293

Linkage Corp. v. Trustees of Boston University, 227, 1608–1610

Linkey v. Medical College of Ohio, 264–265

Linnemeir v. Board of Trustees, Indiana University-Purdue University, 611, 624, 633n

Lipsett v. University of Puerto Rico, 944, 957

Lister v. Hoover, 830

Litman v. George Mason University, 1301, 1312, 1483, 1500

Little v. City of North Miami, 1241

Liu v. Striuli, 951, 953

Livingstone College, 285, 494

Lloyd v. Alpha Phi Alpha & Cornell University, 1091–1092

Lloyd v. Tanner, 55

Local 4501 Communications Workers of America v. Ohio State University (466 N.E.2d 912), 1608

Local 4501 Communications Workers of America v. Ohio State University (494 N.E.2d 1082), 1608

Local 93, International Association of Firefighters v. City of Cleveland, 781n

Locke v. Davey, 68–70, 841

Lockhart v. United States, 852

Loder v. State of New York, 201–202

Loebel v. New York University, In re, 574

Logan v. Bennington College Corp., 47–48

Logan v. Zimmerman Brush Co., 556

Logan Lanes v. Brunswick Corp., 1600–1601

Lombard v. Fireman's Fund Insurance Co., 191

Long v. Board of Trustees, 1622

Long v. Samson, 104–105

Long Island University v. Tappan, 1171

Lopez; United States v., 1298, 1300, 1302–1303

Lorance v. AT&T Technologies, Inc., 103

Loretto Heights College, 493

Louisiana; United States v. (692 F. Supp. 642), 1456

Louisiana; United States v. (751 F. Supp. 606), 1456

Louisiana ex rel. Guste v. United States, 1456

Lovelace v. Southeastern Massachusetts University, 645

Lovell v. Griffin, 1013n

Loving v. Boren, 871–872

Ludwig v. Board of Trustees of Ferris State University, 361

Lueth v. St. Clair County Community College, 1106

L.W. v. Western Golf Association, 200, 882

Lynch v. Donnelly, 71

Lynch v. Indiana State University Board of Trustees, 633n

Lyons v. Salve Regina College, 170

M

Maas v. Cornell University, 321, 473, 482

Mabey v. Reagan, 588, 595

MacKay v. State, 104

MacMurray College v. Wright, 1187

MacPherson v. University of Montevallo, 517

Maczaczyj v. State of New York, 971

Mader v. Health Care Authority, 483–484

Mader v. State of Washington, 484

Madey v. Duke University, 1652

Madsen v. Women's Health Center, 1011–1012

Mahan v. Howell, 1205

Mahavongsanan v. Hill, 727–728

Mailloux v. Kiley, 631n

Maine v. Sterling, 918–919

Mainstream Loudoun v. Board of Trustees of the Loudoun County Library, 868, 872, 875

Maitland v. University of Minnesota, 520

Mallory v. Ohio University, 220

Malone v. Academy of Court Reporting, 1534n

Mandel v. U.S. Department of Health, Education & Welfare, 1490

Mangaroo v. Nelson, 346

Mangla v. Brown University, 731

Manhattan College, 494

Manor Junior College v. Kaller's, Inc., 1612

Maples v. Martin, 568, 674–675, 677

Marbury v. Central State University, 184

Marbury v. Madison, 60

Marcum v. Dahl, 1119

Marder v. Board of Regents of the University of Wisconsin System, 1286

Marin v. University of Puerto Rico, 974

Marjorie Webster Junior College v. District of Columbia Board of Zoning Adjustment, 1173–1174

Marjorie Webster Junior College v. Middle States Association of Colleges & Secondary Schools, 1369, 1535–1536, 1540, 1541, 1543, 1546

Marlboro Corp. v. Association of Independent Colleges & Schools, 1535–1536, 1543–1544

Marlow v. United States Department of Education, 1492–1493

Marsh v. Chambers, 71, 74

Marshall v. Regis Educational Corp., 308–309

Marshall v. State ex rel. Department of Transportation, 877

Marson v. Northwestern State University, 470

Martin v. Guillot, 126

Martin v. Helstad, 753

Martin v. Occupational Safety & Health Review Commission, 949

Martin v. Parrish, 39, 630, 636, 649, 651, 652, 742n, 1018n

Martinez v. Bynum, 833

Mary Gallwey, State ex rel. v. Grimm, 67–68

Marymount College of Virginia, 493

Mason v. State ex rel. Board of Regents of the University of Oklahoma, 224

Mason v. State of Oklahoma, 808

Mason v. Wolf, 1006, 1223

Massachusetts Board of Retirement v. Murgia, 775

Massachusetts Community College Council v. Commonwealth of Massachusetts, 478

Massachusetts School of Law at Andover, Inc. v. American Bar Association, 1548–1549

Mastronito; United States v., 850

Mathews v. Diaz, 834n

Mathews v. Eldridge, 560, 570, 918

Mathis v. Phillips Chevrolet, Inc., 359

Matikas v. University of Dayton, 264

Matthew Bender & Co. & Hyperlaw v. West Publishing Co., 1352

Matthews v. National Collegiate Athletic Association, 1579-1581
Matthews v. Superior Court, 332
Mauriello v. University of Medicine & Dentistry of New Jersey, 985
Mayberry v. Dees, 538
Mayor & City Council of Baltimore v. Mathews, 1490-1491
Mazart v. State, 191, 748, 1110-1114
McCallum v. North Carolina Cooperative Extension Service, 262
McClendon v. City of Columbia, 355
McConnell v. Howard University, 116-117, 473, 481, 532, 654
McCormack v. NCAA, 1568-1569
McCulloch v. PNC Bank, Inc., 1437-1438
McDaniels v. Flick, 560-562
McDonald v. City of West Branch, 299
McDonald v. Hogness, 788
McDonald v. Santa Fe Trail Transportation Co., 760
McElearney v. University of Illinois, 124
McEnroy v. St. Meinrad School of Theology, 489, 714, 716
McEvaddy v. City University of New York, 191
McGann v. H&H Music Co., 313
McGill v. The Regents of the University of California, 539-540
McGlinchy v. Shell Chemical Co., 1571
McGough v. University of San Francisco, 293
McGrath v. University of Alaska, 1287
McGuinness v. Regents of the University of New Mexico, 121
McGuinness v. University of New Mexico School of Medicine, 960-961
MCI Communications Corp. v. American Telephone & Telegraph Co., 1655
McKeesport Hospital v. Accreditation Council for Graduate Medical Education, 1545-1546
McKelvey v. Pierce, 57
McKelvy v. Diocese of Camden, 228
McLachlan v. Tacoma Community College District No. 22, 273
McLaughlin v. Richland Shoe Co., 306
McLemore, State ex rel. v. Clarksville School of Theology, 1265-1266

McLendon v. Morton, 553
McMaster Construction, Inc. v. Board of Regents of Oklahoma Colleges, 1613-1614
Medical Institute of Minnesota v. National Association of Trade & Technical Schools, 1541-1542, 1544
Medical Society of South Carolina v. Medical University of South Carolina, 1627
Medina v. City & County of Denver, 351
Medlock v. Board of Trustees of the University of Massachusetts, 1328
Mehta, In re, 846
Meling, In re, 845
Mellen v. Bunting, 73-75
Melvin v. Union College, 989
Memphis, City of v. Alpha Beta Welfare Association, 1191
Memphis Community School District v. Stachura, 121-122, 240
Mendez v. Reynolds, 184-185
Mentavlos v. Anderson, 46n, 51-52, 748
Mercer v. Duke University, 1139
Mercy Catholic Medical Center v. Thompson, 1401, 1443
Meritor Savings Bank, FSB v. Vinson, 750
Merwine v. Board of Trustees for State Institutions of Higher Learning, 1532
Messina v. Burden, 336
Metropolitan Life Insurance v. Taylor, 313
Meyer v. Burger King Corporation, 325
Meyer v. Nebraska, 41
MGM Studios, Inc. v. Grokster, Ltd., 1341
Miami Student, State ex rel. v. Miami University, 1037-1038
Miami University; United States v., 1038, 1436
Miami Wrestling Club v. Miami University, 1138
Michaelson v. Cox, 830
Michigan v. VanTubbergen, 877
Microsoft; United States v., 711-713
Middlebury College Sales & Use Tax, In re, 1249, 1637
Middletown v. Hartman, 311
Midwest Research Institute v. United States, 1636, 1653
Milbouer v. Keppler, 591
Milkovich v. Lorain Journal Co., 338
Miller v. California, 1107-1108
Miller v. Loyola University of New Orleans, 217

Miller v. Sonoma County Junior College District, 776
Miller v. State, 880-881
Miller v. Washington State Community College, 99-100
Miller Brewing Co. v. Brewery Workers Local Union No. 9, 138
Miller ex rel. Miller v. HCA, Inc., 1291
Millien v. Colby College, 991
Milton S. Hershey Medical Center of the Pennsylvania State University, In re, 1289
Milwaukee Journal v. Board of Regents of the University of Wisconsin System, 1283
Minger v. Green, 332
Mink v. University of Chicago, 1291
Minnesota State Board for Community Colleges v. Knight, 289, 497-498, 666
Missert v. Trustees of Boston University, 1324n
Mississippi Gay Alliance v. Goudelock, 1102
Mississippi State Alumni Association, Inc. v. Commissioner, 1419n
Mississippi University for Women v. Hogan, 763-764
Mitchell v. Helms, 62-63, 64
Mitsubishi Motors Corp. v. Soler Chrysler-Plymouth, Inc., 1645
Mittra v. University of Medicine & Dentistry of New Jersey, 729
Mohawk Book Co. v. State University of New York, 1284
Molpus v. Fortune, 1215
Monell v. Department of Social Services of the City of New York, 232-233, 239-240
Monroe v. Pape, 1562
Montefiore Hospital & Medical Center & New York State Federation of Physicians & Dentists, 493
Moore v. Board of Regents of the University of the State of New York, 1253-1254, 1259
Moore v. Regents of the University of California, 1290
Moore v. University of Notre Dame, 219
Moore v. Vanderloo, 214
Moosa v. State Personnel Board, 567
Moose Lodge v. Irvis, 43n
Morales; United States v., 870, 1396-1397
Moresco v. Clark, 973, 976
Morgan v. American University, 267, 566

Morgantown, City of v. West Virginia Board of Regents, 1199, 1638

Morgantown, City of v. West Virginia University Medical Corporation, 245–246

Morris v. Nowotny, 168

Morris; United States v., 1385

Morrison v. Kappa Alpha Psi Fraternity, 209, 1090–1091

Morrison; United States v., 1298, 1303, 1304

Morse v. Regents of the University of Colorado, 748, 950n

Mostaghim v. Fashion Institute of Technology, 938

Motor Vehicle Manufacturers Association v. State Farm Mutual Automobile Insurance Co., 1443

Motz v. Johnson, 1093

Motzkin v. Trustees of Boston University, 515–516

Mt. Healthy City School District Board of Education v. Doyle, 691–692, 694, 696–698, 790n

Mt. Sinai School of Medicine v. American Tobacco Co., In re, 709

Mull v. Oregon Institute of Technology, 973

Mullins v. Pine Manor College, 194, 880

Mumford v. Godfried, 675

Murdy v. Bureau of Blindness & Visual Services, 895

Murphy v. Duquesne University of the Holy Ghost, 135, 574–575

Murphy v. Office of Vocational & Educational Services for Individuals With Disabilities, 894–895

Murphy v. United Parcel Service, 961

Murray v. New York University College of Dentistry, 943

Murrell v. Mount St. Clare College, 881–882

Murtaugh v. Emory University, 476

Muskovitz v. Lubbers, 704

Myles v. Regents of the University of California, 297

N

NAACP v. Alabama ex rel. Patterson, 619

NAACP v. Button, 612, 1025

Nabozny v. Podlesny, 958

Namenwirth v. Regents of the University of Wisconsin, 514

Napolitano v. Trustees of Princeton University, 735, 992–993

Naranjo, In re, 845

Nash v. Auburn University, 978

Nash v. Trustees of Boston University, 267

Nasson College, In re, 1553

National Board of Medical Examiners; Doe v., 775

National Coalition for Students With Disabilities Education & Legal Defense Fund v. Allen, 1314

National Coalition for Students With Disabilities Education & Legal Defense Fund v. Gilmore, 895–896

National Collegiate Athletic Association. See NCAA

National Endowment for the Arts v. Finley, 1447–1448

National Labor Relations Board v. See name of opposing party

National League of Cities v. Usery, 1302

National Movement for the Student Vote v. Regents of the University of California, 1204

National Society of Professional Engineers v. United States, 1369–1370, 1547, 1571

National Treasury Employees Union; United States v., 610–611, 661

National Treasury Employees Union v. Von Raabe, 268

National Wrestling Coaches Association v. Department of Education, 101, 1138–1139, 1440–1441, 1530

Native American Heritage Commission v. Board of Trustees of the California State University, 627

NCAA v. Board of Regents of the University of Oklahoma, 1374–1375, 1566–1567, 1571, 1632

NCAA v. Miller, Governor, State of Nevada, 1564–1565

NCAA v. Roberts, 1565

NCAA v. Smith, 1573–1574

NCAA v. Tarkanian, 1546, 1562–1563

NCAA v. Yeo, 1116–1119

Neal v. California State University, 1137–1138

Near v. State of Minnesota, 1112

Nebraska Press Association v. Stuart, 1008

Nedder v. Rivier College, 516

Neighborhood Action Coalition v. City of Canton, 1496

Neilson; Commonwealth v., 863–864

Neiman v. Yale University, 576

Nelson v. Pima Community College, 329

Nemani v. St. Louis University, 223

Nemser; State v., 866

Neo Gen Screening, Inc. v. University of Massachusetts, 1373–1374

Nero v. Kansas State University, 200, 883

Nevada Department of Human Resources v. Hibbs, 316, 1306, 1311

Newark, City of v. University of Delaware, 1168

Newberry v. East Texas State University, 515

New Era Publications International v. Henry Holt & Co., 1339

New Jersey v. T.L.O., 862n

New Jersey Board of Higher Education v. Shelton College, 1264–1265

New Jersey Chamber of Commerce v. Hughey, 304

New Jersey Coalition Against War in the Middle East v. J.M.B. Realty Corp., 1228

New Jersey State College Locals v. State Board of Higher Education, 499

Newman v. Sathyavaglswaran, 1290

Newport, City of v. Fact Concerts, Inc., 240

New York v. Coury, 808–809

New York v. Ferber, 869, 1388

New York v. United States, 1298

New York Association of Career Schools v. State Education Department, 1261

New York Botanical Garden v. Board of Standards & Appeals & Fordham University, In re, 1180

New York Institute of Technology v. LeBoutillier, 1174

New York State Board of Law Examiners v. Bartlett, 961

New York Times v. Sullivan, 338–339, 1108n, 1551n

New York University, 302, 495

New York University; Doe v., 771

New York University v. Taylor, 1197

Nicholas v. Pennsylvania State University, 564, 696

Nicholson v. Northeast Louisiana University, 199

Nieswand v. Cornell University, 881

Nigro v. Research College of Nursing, 217

Niles v. Board of Regents of the University System of Georgia, 202

Nisbet v. Bucher, 1094

NLRB v. See name of opposing party

Noah v. AOL Time Warner, Inc., 874

Nollan v. California Coastal Commission, 1170

Norman-Bloodshaw v. Lawrence Berkeley Laboratory, 269–270

Norris v. State Council of Higher Education, 1453

North v. West Virginia Board of Regents, 753–754

North Carolina v. Pendleton, 877

North Dakota v. North Central Association of Colleges & Secondary Schools, 1534

North Haven Board of Education v. Bell, 1473

Northwestern University v. City of Arden Hills, 1171

Northwestern University v. City of Evanston, 1170

Norwood v. Harrison, 45n

Nova Southeastern University v. Gross, 204–205

Nova University v. Board of Governors of the University of North Carolina, 1270–1271

Nova University v. Educational Institution Licensure Commission, 1271–1272

Nyquist v. Jean-Marie Mauclet, 833–835

Nzuve v. Castleton State College, 918

O

O'Brien v. New England Telephone & Telegraph Co., 105

O'Brien; United States v., 1431

O'Connell v. State of New Jersey, 194

O'Connor v. Davis, 1482

O'Connor v. Ortega, 612–613

Oda v. State of Washington, 519

Oden v. Northern Marianas College, 951–952

Ohio v. Spingola, 999, 1218, 1223

Ohio Civil Rights Commission v. Case Western Reserve University, 773–774

Ohio Dominican College v. Krone, 534–535

Ohralick v. Ohio State Bar Association, 1232

Oja v. Grand Chapter of Theta Chi Fraternity, Inc., 1094

Okruhlik v. University of Arkansas ex rel. May, 1311

Olin v. Wakinekona, 555

Ollman v. Toll, 696

Olsson v. Board of Higher Education of the City of New York, 184, 934–935

Olsson v. Indiana University Board of Trustees, 218

164 Mulberry Street Corp. v. Columbia University, 221, 1318n

Online Policy Group v. Diebold, Inc., 875

Oona v. McCaffrey, 956

Orange v. District of Columbia, 275–276

Oregon Health Sciences University, State ex. rel. v. Haas, 110

Oregon State University Alumni Association v. Commissioner, 1419n, 1635, 1636

Organiscak v. Cleveland State University, 804

Orin v. Barclay, 878, 1218, 1222–1223

Orozco-Santillan; United States v., 870

Ortwein v. Mackey, 550

Osborn & Center for Equal Opportunity v. Board of Regents of the University of Wisconsin System, 1285

Osborne v. Johnson, 110

Osborne v. Stone, 566

Oshkosh, City of v. Winkler, 919

Ostasz v. Medical College of Ohio, 340

Osteen v. Henley, 918

Ostrander v. Duggan, 1092n, 1096

Ottgen v. Clover Park Technical College, 730

Owasso Independent School District v. Falvo, 1034n

Owen v. City of Independence, 239n, 241

Owens v. Storehouse, 313

P

Pace v. Bogalusa City School Board, 819, 1312

Pace v. Hymas, 581–582

Pacific Gas & Electric Co. v. State Energy Resources Conservation & Development Commission, 1297n

Packer Collegiate Institute v. University of the State of New York, 1262

Pahulu v. University of Kansas, 1140–1141

Paine v. Board of Regents of the University of Texas System, 914–915

Palmer v. District Board of Trustees of St. Petersburg Junior College, 524n

Panarella v. Birenbaum, 1112

Papadikis v. Iowa State University of Science & Technology, 277

Papish v. Board of Curators of the University of Missouri, 738, 1004, 1107

Paradise; United States v., 796

Parate v. Isibor, 645–646, 653

PARC v. Pennsylvania, 768

Parham, In re, 847

Parish v. NCAA, 1561

Parker v. Brown, 1369

Parker v. Flook, 1356, 1357

Parraway v. Andrews University, 847

Parsons College v. North Central Association of Colleges & Secondary Schools, 1535–1536, 1538–1540, 1541–1542, 1543

Passonno v. State University of New York at Albany, 277

Patsy v. Board of Regents of the State of Florida, 104n, 240–241, 576n

Patterson v. Southwestern Baptist Theological Seminary, 489–490

Pauk v. Board of Trustees of the City University of New York, 102–103, 118–119

Paul v. Davis, 550n

Paulsen v. Golden Gate University, 755

Peacock v. Board of Regents of University & State Colleges of Arizona, 578

Peck v. University Residence Committee of Kansas State University, 828, 831

Pederson v. Louisiana State University, 818, 1135, 1136, 1500

Peel v. Salliemae Servicing-HEAL Loan, 845

Peirce Junior College v. Schumaker, 1179

Pelkowski, In re, 845

Penn v. Harris, 879

Pennhurst State School & Hospital v. Halderman, 1299–1300, 1308

Pennsylvania v. Croushore, 877

Pennsylvania v. Downing, 1212

Pennsylvania v. Tate, 56, 1228

Pennsylvania v. Union Gas, 1308–1309

Pennsylvania State University v. Commissioner, Department of Labor & Industry, 704

Pennsylvania State University v. University Orthopedics, 1364–1365

People v. See name of opposing party

People ex rel. See name of party

People for the Ethical Treatment of Animals v. Institutional Animal Care & Use Committee of the University of Oregon, 100–101, 1327

Perez v. City University of New York, 188, 1277

Perfect 10, Inc. v. Cybernet Ventures, Inc., 1348
Perry v. Sindermann, 36, 470, 547, 549, 605, 606n, 1584
Perry Education Association v. Perry Local Educators' Association, 292, 997n, 1000
Petaluma City School District; Doe v., 749, 947
Peters v. Jenney, 1483
Peterson v. San Francisco Community College District, 884
Pfaff v. Columbia-Greene Community College, 104, 912–913
PGA Tour, Inc. v. Martin, 1383–1384
Phelps v. Board of Education of West New York, 479
Phelps v. President & Trustees of Colby College, 1080
Phelps v. Washburn University of Topeka, 753
Philadelphia v. New Jersey, 1268
Philadelphia, City of; United States v., 1164–1165, 1297
Phillip v. Fairfield University & The National Collegiate Athletic Association, 1573
Phillips v. Martin Marietta, 503
Phillips v. Moore, 364
Physicians Committee for Responsible Medicine v. National Institutes of Health, 1327–1328
Physicians National House Staff Association v. Fanning, 302
Piarowski v. Illinois Community College, 611–612, 625, 726
Piazzola v. Watkins, 862, 865
Pickering v. Board of Education, 350, 606, 607, 621, 1239–1240
Pickings v. Bruce, 1240
Pierce v. Ortho Pharmaceutical, 328
Pierce v. Smith, 268
Pierce v. Society of Sisters, 41
Pike v. Bruce Church, 1269
Pikulin v. City University of New York, 238
Pi Lambda Phi Fraternity v. University of Pittsburgh, 1082–1083
Pima Community College v. Arizona Department of Economic Security, 327
Pioneer Roofing Co. v. Mardian Construction Co., 1595
Piotrowski v. City of Houston, 355
Pitock v. State, 100
Pitre v. Louisiana Tech University, 198–199
Pitt News v. Pappert, 1106
Pittsburgh Press Co. v. Pittsburgh Commission on Human Relations, 1105

Planned Parenthood of Columbia/Willamette, Inc. v. American Coalition of Life Advocates, 870–871
Planned Parenthood of Southeastern Pennsylvania v. Casey, 1289
Plyler v. Doe, 778, 837
Podberesky v. Kirwan, 789, 823–825
Poe v. Leonard, 337
Polaski v. Clark, 831–832
Police Department v. Mosley, 1024, 1071
Polishook v. City University of New York, In re, 180
Pomona College v. The Superior Court of Los Angeles County, 577
Potemra v. Ping, 559
Powe v. Miles, 42
Powell v. Syracuse University, 131, 502
Power v. Summers, 241, 610, 1308
Prairie View A&M University of Texas v. Mitchell, 192
Pred v. Board of Instruction of Dade County, Florida, 631n
Presbyterian Church v. Hull Church, 59n
Presbyterian Medical Center of the University of Pennsylvania Health System v. Shalala, 1401
President & Directors of Georgetown College v. District of Columbia Board of Zoning Adjustment, 1176
President & Directors of Georgetown College v. Hughes, 194
Preyer v. Dartmouth College, 1481
Prime v. Beta Gamma Chapter of Pi Kappa Alpha, 1095
Princeton University & State of New Jersey v. Schmid, 1227n, 1228, 1246
Princeton University Press v. Borough of Princeton, 1192–1193
Princeton University Press v. Michigan Document Services, Inc., 1337
Printz v. United States, 1298
Proctor & Gamble Co. v. Swilly, 711
Procunier v. Navarette, 348
Property Owners Association v. Board of Zoning Appeals, 1172
Pro Schools, Inc. v. Riley, 851
Prostrollo v. University of South Dakota, 854, 859
PruneYard Shopping Center v. Robins, 55–56
Prusack v. State, 733
Pryor v. NCAA, 1576

Psi Upsilon v. University of Pennsylvania, 1085–1086
Pugel v. Board of Trustees of the University of Illinois, 981–982
Pugh v. See's Candies, Inc., 265
Purdie v. University of Utah, 776
Pushkin v. Regents of the University of Colorado, 770, 968, 1496
Putnam v. Keller, 551
Pyeatte v. Board of Regents of the University of Oklahoma, 1243–1244

Q

Quern v. Jordan, 232–233
Quilichini v. Universidad Católica, 685–686, 687
Quinn v. Mississippi State University, 229
Quinn v. Sigma Rho Chapter, 1090n
Quinnipiac College; NLRB v., 280, 289

R

Rabel v. Illinois Wesleyan University, 197, 882
Radcliffe College v. City of Cambridge, 1173
Rader v. Johnston, 856–857
Ragsdale v. Wolverine Worldwide, Inc., 315–316
Railroad Commission of Texas v. Pullman, 100n
Raines v. Haverford College, 265
Rajender v. University of Minnesota, 514
Ramos v. California Committee of Bar Examiners, 1263–1264
Rancho Santiago College; People v., 1178
Randi W. v. Muroc Joint Unified School District, 221, 343–344
Ranney v. Instituto Pontificio Delle Maestre Filippini, 1177
Rashed v. State of New York, 193
R.A.V. v. City of St. Paul, 1019–1020, 1022–1023, 1047, 1238n
Ravindranathan v. Virginia Commonwealth University, 832–833
Ray v. Wilmington College, 915
R.B. Plummer Memorial Loan Fund Trust, In re, 810
Recording Industry Association of America v. Verizon Internet Services, Inc. (351 F.3d 1229), 1350
Recording Industry Association of America v. Verizon Internet Services, Inc. (240 F. Supp. 2d 24, 257 F. Supp. 2d 244), 1350

Red & Black Publishing Co. v. Board of Regents, 1280, 1283
Regan v. State, 1150–1151
Regan v. Taxation With Representation, 1448
Regan v. Time, Inc., 1243
Regensburger v. City of Bowling Green, Ohio, 1206
Regents of the University of California, In re, 1652
Regents of the University of California v. Bakke, 626n, 782, 785–788, 1471, 1475
Regents of the University of California v. City of Santa Monica, 1169
Regents of the University of California v. Doe, 225, 236n
Regents of the University of California v. Eli Lilly & Co., 1652
Regents of the University of California v. Public Employment Relations Board, 292, 301
Regents of the University of California v. Superior Court, 838–839
Regents of the University of Colorado v. K.D.I. Precision Products, Inc., 1646–1647
Regents of the University of Michigan v. Ewing, 130, 131–132, 564, 626, 929, 1584
Regents of the University of Michigan v. Michigan Employment Relations Commission, 1258
Regents of the University of Michigan v. State of Michigan, 1255–1256, 1257
Regents of the University of Minnesota v. Chicago & North Western Transportation Co., 1249–1250
Regents of the University of Minnesota v. Chief Industries, Inc., 1602–1603
Regents of the University of Minnesota v. NCAA, 1116
Regents of the University System of Georgia; State v., 1623
Regions Hospital v. Shalala, 1400
Rehor v. Case Western Reserve University, 271
Reilly v. Daly, 117–118, 127n, 977
Reimer v. Champion Healthcare, 310
Rendell-Baker v. Kohn, 43–46, 1544, 1562
Reno v. American Civil Liberties Union, 659–660, 872n, 873, 1387, 1389–1393
Renshaw, In re, 846
Rensing v. Indiana State University Board of Trustees, 324

Rensselaer Polytechnic Institute v. Commissioner, 1636–1637
Rensselaer Society of Engineers v. Rensselaer Polytechnic Institute, In re, 989, 1081
Reproductive Rights Network v. President of the University of Massachusetts, 1216–1217
Retired Adjunct Professors of the State of Rhode Island v. Almond, 478–479
Revell v. Lidov, 98
Reynolds v. Sims, 1205
Rhode Island Department of Environmental Management v. United States, 1380
Richards v. League of United Latin American Citizens, 760
Richards of Rockford, Inc. v. Pacific Gas & Electric Co., 708
Richardson v. Blanton, 1453
Richardson v. McKnight, 878
Richmond, City of v. J.A. Croson Co., 787–788, 796, 800, 1614–1615
Rieder v. State University of New York, 576
Riggin v. Board of Trustees of Ball State University, 115–116, 529
Riggio v. Burns, 1274n
Riggs; United States v., 1394
Rivera v. Hospital Universitario, 335
R.L.R. v. Prague Public School District I-103, 947n
Roberson, In re, 845
Roberts v. Colorado State Board of Agriculture, 1133, 1134n
Roberts v. Haragan, 999, 1006, 1025–1026
Roberts v. United States Jaycees, 1082
Robertson v. State of Louisiana, 199
Robins v. PruneYard Shopping Center, 55
Robinson v. University of Akron School of Law, 960, 1383
Rocha v. Pi Kappa Alpha, 1095
Rockland Institute v. Association of Independent Colleges & Schools, 1536n, 1541–1542
Roe v. Cheyenne Mountain Conference Resort, 269
Roemer v. Board of Public Works, 63–64, 1071
Rogers v. Lodge, 782
Rogers v. New York University, 299–300
Roklina v. Skidmore College, 541
Rome, City of v. United States, 1475
Romer v. Evans, 1069
Rosado v. Wyman, 1029n

Rosa H. v. San Elizario Independent School District, 947–948
Rosenberg v. Merrill Lynch, Pierce, Fenner & Smith, Inc., 274
Rosenberger v. Rector & Visitors of University of Virginia, 64, 619, 634, 662, 738–740, 871, 901, 997n, 998–999, 1001, 1014n, 1051n, 1054, 1074–1078, 1099–1100, 1153, 1238n, 1446–1448
Rosenstock v. Board of Governors of the University of North Carolina, 777
Rosenthal v. Webster University, 807, 926–927
Ross v. Creighton University, 213–214, 1126–1127
Ross v. Medical University of South Carolina, 110–112, 150
Ross v. St. Augustine's College, 343, 937
Ross Learning, Inc. v. Riley, 851
Rothbard v. Colgate University, 1092
Rothstein v. City University of New York, 1212n
Roufaiel v. Ithaca College, 541–542
Rounds v. Oregon State Board of Higher Education, 236, 238–239, 1058, 1065
Rowe v. Laidlaw Transit, Inc., 310
Rumsfeld v. FAIR, 1431
Runyon v. McCrary, 760, 1305
Russell v. Salve Regina College, 932–933
Russell v. Yale University, 181
Russo v. Nassau County Community College, 1284
Rust v. Fitzhugh, 1594
Rust v. Sullivan, 892, 1443–1447
Rutan v. Republican Party of Illinois, 612
Rutcosky v. Board of Trustees of Community College District No. 18, 544
Rutgers, The State University v. Piluso, 1168–1169
Ryles v. Durham County Hospital Corp., 322

S

Sackman v. Alfred University, 576, 577–578
Sacred Heart University, 494
Saenz v. Roe, 778, 830
St. Agnes Hospital v. Riddick, 1289, 1544–1545
St. Joseph's College, 285
St. Martin Evangelical Lutheran Church v. South Dakota, 1414n
St. Mary's Honor Center v. Hicks, 503

St. Norbert College Foundation v.
McCormick, 1594
St. Paul-Ramsey Medical Center v.
Shalala, 1400n
St. Thomas University, 493
Salehpour v. University of
Tennessee, 740n, 1016
Salem College & Academy v.
Employment Division, 326
Salinger v. Random House, 1339
Salvador v. Bennett, 772, 1493
Salve Regina College v. Zoning
Board of Review of City of
Newport, 1177
Samaan v. Trustees of California
State University & Colleges,
117, 129n
Samuel v. University of Pittsburgh,
107, 827
San Antonio Independent School
District v. Rodriguez, 826
San Diego, City of v. Roe, 608
Sandoval v. Board of Regents of the
University & Community Col-
lege System of Nevada, 1276
San Filippo v. Bongiovanni,
533–534, 612
San Francisco Labor Council v.
Regents of the University of
California, 1256–1257
San Jose Christian College v. City
of Morgan Hill, 60n
Santa Fe Independent School
District v. Doe, 73
Santa Rosa Junior College v.
Workers' Compensation
Appeals Board, 325
Sarkisian Brothers, Inc. v.
Hartnett, 1605
Sarvis v. Vermont State Colleges,
267
Saucier v. Katz, 348, 349, 878
Scallet v. Rosenblum, 634–635,
649, 650, 675–676, 692,
697–698
Scanlan v. Texas A&M University,
356
Scarce v. United States, 711
Scelsa v. City University of New
York, 524
Schaer v. Brandeis University,
991
Schaper v. City of Huntsville, 562
Scharf v. Regents of the University
of California, 705
Schaumburg v. Citizens for Better
Environment, 1237
Schenck v. Pro-Choice Network of
Western New York, 1011–1012
Scherer v. Curators of the Univer-
sity of Missouri, 98
Scheuer v. Rhodes, 347
Scheuller v. Board of Adjustment,
1172
Schier v. Temple University, 47,
50n

Schieszler v. Ferrum College, 211
Schiff v. Williams, 1101–1102
Schmid; State v., 46n, 56, 1212,
1224–1228, 1246
Schneider v. State of New Jersey,
1013
School Board of Nassau County v.
Arline, 1467
School District of Abington
Township v. Schempp,
57–58
Schornstein v. New Jersey Division
of Vocational Rehabilitation
Services, 894
Schrier v. University of Colorado,
679n
SCM Corp. v. Xerox Corp., 1655
Scott v. State, 1148
Scott v. Western State University
College of Law, 963
Seal v. Morgan, 923
Seare v. University of Utah School
of Medicine, 735
Searle v. Regents of the University
of California, 187–188
Seidlitz; United States v., 1394
Selective Service System v.
Minnesota Public Interest
Research Group, 815
Self v. Texas A&M University,
354–356
Seminole Tribe v. Florida, 1298,
1303, 1308–1309, 1351,
1498–1499
Serbian Orthodox Diocese v.
Milivojevich, 59n
Seton Hall University Faculty
Association v. Seton Hall
University, 286
Settle v. Dickson County School
Board, 744
Seus v. John Nuveen & Co., 274
SE/Z Construction, L.L.C. v. Idaho
State University, 1613
Shamloo v. Mississippi State
Board of Trustees, 1002, 1004,
1007
Shapiro v. Columbia Union
National Bank & Trust Co.,
52, 810
Shapp v. Sloan, 1247–1248
Sharick v. Southeastern University
of the Health Sciences, Inc.,
733
Sharif by Salahuddin v. New York
State Education Department,
767, 820
Sharik v. Southeastern University
of the Health Sciences, 930n
Sharon v. City of Newton, 159
Sharp v. Zoning Hearing Board of
the Township of Radnor, 1179
Shaw v. Board of Trustees, 630
Shaw v. Reno, 1205
Shea v. Emmanuel College, 328
Shearer v. Lambert, 218

Sheet Metal Workers v. EEOC, 800
Shelton v. Tucker, 618
Shelton College v. State Board of
Education, 1258, 1264n
Shepard v. Irving, 960
Sherbert v. Verner, 1266
Sheridan v. Trustees of Columbia
University, 848
Sherman v. Community Consoli-
dated School District, 71
Sherman v. Curators of the Univer-
sity of Missouri, 236–237
Sherman College of Straight
Chiropractic v. U.S. Commis-
sioner of Education, 1558
Shimer v. Bowling Green State
University, 198
Shin v. MIT, 211, 335
Shlien v. Board of Regents
of University of Nebraska,
223
Sholvin v. University of
Medicine & Dentistry of
New Jersey, 681–682
Shreveport Professional Chapter of
the Society of Professional
Journalists v. Louisiana State
University, 1036–1037
Shriners Hospitals for Crippled
Children v. First Security Bank
of Utah, 180–181
Shurben v. Dollar Rent-A-Car, 204
Shuttlesworth v. Birmingham,
1010n
Siblerud v. Colorado State Board
of Agriculture, 986
Sicard v. University of Dayton,
1151
Siegel v. National Periodical
Publications, Inc., 1344
Siegert v. Gilley, 348, 930
Sierra Club v. Commissioner,
1419n
Sigall, State ex rel. v. Aetna Clean-
ing Contractors of Cleveland,
Inc., 1607
Siler-Khodr v. University of Texas
Health Science Center San
Antonio, 520
Silva v. University of New
Hampshire, 637, 641–642,
649–651
Silverman v. University of
Colorado, 182–183, 185
Silvers v. Associated Technical
Institute, Inc., 204n
Simon & Schuster, Inc. v. Members
of New York State Crime
Victims Board, 1448
Simonson v. Iowa State University,
570
Sinn v. The Daily Nebraskan,
1102
Sipfle v. Board of Governors of
the University of North
Carolina, 186

Sirohi v. Lee, 215
Sisters of Holy Cross v. Brookline, 1173
Siu v. Johnson, 554–555
Skehan v. Board of Trustees of Bloomsburg State College, 544, 561, 578
Skehan v. State System of Higher Education, 235
Skinner v. Railway Labor Executives Association, 268, 1142, 1143–1144
Skorin-Kapov v. State University of New York at Stony Brook, 557
Slatkin v. University of Redlands, 541
Slaughter v. Brigham Young University, 728, 924, 933
Slovinec v. DePaul University, 816, 848, 1437
Small v. Juniata College, 262
Smith v. Alabama Aviation & Technical College, 120
Smith v. Atkins, 341–342
Smith v. Board of Regents of the University of Houston, 828–829
Smith v. California, 1007
Smith v. City University of New York, 248
Smith v. Duquesne University, 47
Smith v. Gardner & Board of Regents, San Jacinto College District, 222–223
Smith v. Goguen, 1007
Smith v. Hennepin County Technical Center, 957
Smith v. NCAA, 1479, 1570–1571, 1573–1574
Smith; People v., 877
Smith v. Regents of the University of California, 1058
Smith v. State, 1661
Smith v. University of Texas, 198
Smith v. University of Washington Law School (233 F.3d 1188), 791n
Smith v. University of Washington Law School (392 F.3d 367), 791n, 801
Smith v. Virginia Commonwealth University, 520
Smith v. Wade, 353
Snyder, In re, 711
Sobel v. Yeshiva University, 518–519
Sodergren v. The Johns Hopkins University Applied Physics Laboratory, 339
Soglin v. Kauffman, 922, 923
Sohmer v. Kinnard, 915
Sola v. Lafayette College, 470
Solo Cup Co. v. Federal Insurance Co., 157
Soni v. Board of Trustees of University of Tennessee, 550

Sonnichsen v. Baylor University, 266
Sony Corp. of America v. Universal City Studios, Inc., 1340
Soong v. University of Hawaii, 930
Soper v. Hoben, 953, 1464
Sophianopoulous v. McCormick, 340
Sorey v. Kellett, 336
Sosna v. Iowa, 830
Souders v. Lucero, 1221–1222
South Carolina v. Baker, 1301
South Carolina v. Katzenbach, 1305
South Dakota v. Dole, 1299
South Dakota Board of Regents v. Meierhenry, 142
South Dakota Education Association v. South Dakota Board of Regents, 294–295
South Dakota Sigma Chapter House Association v. Clay County, 1190
Southeastern Community College v. Davis, 769–770, 965, 1467–1468
Southeastern Promotions v. Conrad, 1010n, 1107
Southeastern University of the Health Sciences, Inc. v. Sharick, 733
Southern Christian Leadership Conference v. Supreme Court, 1241–1242
Southern Illinois University Foundation v. Booker, 1185, 1188
Southern Junior College; State ex rel. various citizens, 1627–1628
Southern Pacific Terminal Co. v. Interstate Commerce Commission, 101
South Jersey Catholic School Teachers Organization v. St. Teresa of the Infant Jesus Church Elementary School, 286
South Texas College of Law and Texas A&M University, In re, 174
South Texas College of Law and Texas A&M University v. Texas Higher Education Coordinating Board, 1254–1255
Southwest Center for Biological Diversity v. U.S.D.A., 711
Southworth v. Board of Regents of University of Wisconsin System, 1058–1065
Southworth v. Grebe, 1059
Spartacus Youth League v. Board of Trustees of Illinois Industrial University, 1015, 1098n
Spath v. NCAA, 1564

Spencer v. St. John's University, 493
Spire, State ex rel. v. Conway, 1242
Spring Branch I.S.D. v. Stamos, 1118–1119
Spring Valley Wesley Heights Citizens Association v. District of Columbia Board of Zoning Adjustment, 1180n
Spuler v. Pickar, 541
Stacy v. Williams, 1003, 1214–1215
Staheli v. Smith, 337
Stanley v. Big Eight Conference, 1563
Stanley v. Magrath, 1098–1099
Stanton v. Tulane University, 265
Stanton v. University of Maine System, 881
Starns v. Malkerson, 826, 829
Starsky v. Williams, 683–684, 688–689
Star Tribune Co. v. University of Minnesota Board of Regents, 1279–1280
State v. See name of opposing party
State Board for Community Colleges v. Olson, 631n
State ex rel. See name of party
State Street Bank & Trust Co. v. Signature Financial Group, Inc., 1357
State System of Higher Education v. State College & University Professional Association, 139
Statewide Oilfield Construction, Inc., d/b/a Golden State School, In re, 1554
Staton v. Miami University, 703
Stearns v. Mariani, 1163
Steel v. Industrial Development Board of Metropolitan Government of Nashville, 66
Steelworkers v. American Manufacturing Co., 137n
Steelworkers v. Enterprise Wheel & Car Corp., 137n
Steelworkers v. Warrior & Gulf Navigation, 137n
Stein v. Kent State University Board of Trustees, 538
Stephens v. Roane State Community College, 1288
Stephens Institute; NLRB v., 493
Stepp v. Review Board of the Indiana Employment Security Division, 327
Stern v. Lucy Webb Hayes National Training School for Deaconnesses & Missionaries, 175–178
Stern v. Trustees of Columbia University, 525–526
Steward Machine Co. v. Davis, 1299, 1300

Stockinger v. Feather River Community College, 205

Stoll v. New York State College of Veterinary Medicine at Cornell University, 1282

Stone by Stone v. Cornell University, 42n, 56

Strank v. Mercy Hospital of Johnstown, 36–37

Stratton v. Kent State University, 730

Student Association of the University of Wisconsin-Milwaukee v. Baum, 188, 1050

Student Government Association v. Board of Trustees of the University of Massachusetts, 900–901

Student House, Inc. v. Board of Regents of Regency Universities, 186–187, 189

Student Loan Fund of Idaho, Inc. v. U.S. Department of Education, 815n

Students Against Apartheid Coalition v. O'Neil, 1007–1008

Subryan v. Regents of the University of Colorado, 264

Sugano v. University of Washington, 556–557

Sullivan v. Washington, 336

Summers v. Howard University, 310–311

Sunshine Books, Ltd. v. Temple University, 1632–1633

Susan M v. New York Law School, 935–936, 938

Sutton v. Providence St. Joseph Medical Center, 60

Sutton v. United Air Lines, 961

Swain v. Wiley College, 228–229

Swanson v. University of Cincinnati, 962

Swanson v. University of Hawaii Professional Assembly, 291

Swanson v. Wabash College, 1151

Swartley v. Hoffner, 229

Swartz v. Scruton, 567

Sweezy v. New Hampshire, 617–618, 626, 647, 738, 1313

Sword v. Fox, 923

Symm v. United States, 1200

T

Tacka v. Georgetown University, 218, 481

Talley v. California, 1013n, 1015

Tanaka v. University of Southern California, 1571

Tanberg v. Weld County Sheriff, 772, 1467

Tanford v. Brand, 71–72

Tanja H. v. Regents of the University of California, 882

Tanner v. Oregon Health Sciences University, 124–125

Tarasoff v. Regents of the University of California, 334–335, 925

Tarkanian v. NCAA, 1562

Tatum v. National Collegiate Athletic Association, 1578–1581

Tau Kappa Epsilon; Commonwealth v., 1208

Taylor v. St. Vincent's Medical Center, 304

Taylor v. Wake Forest University, 1124–1125

Tayyari v. New Mexico State University, 778, 835

T.D. v. New York State Office of Mental Health, 1290–1291

Teamsters v. Lucas Flour Co., 293

Teamsters v. University of Vermont, 289

Tedeschi v. Wagner College, 728n, 972

Teichgraeber v. Memorial Union Corporation of Emporia State University, 249

Teitel v. University of Houston Board of Regents, 829

Temple Terrace, City of v. Hillsborough Association, 1167–1168

Temple University v. Tsokas, 1365

Temple University v. Unemployment Compensation Board of Review, 327

Tennessee v. Lane, 1306–1307, 1309n, 1311

Tennessee Student Assistance Corporation v. Hood, 844

Terminiello v. Chicago, 1003

Terrell v. University of Texas System Police, 671

Texas v. Boyd, 914

Texas v. Johnson, 995, 1025

Texas v. Lesage, 790n, 1499n

Texas; United States v., 1200, 1312

Texas A&M University v. Bishop, 207

Texas Faculty Association v. University of Texas at Dallas, 591–592

Texas Farm Bureau v. Commissioner, 1419n

Texas Tech University Health Sciences Center v. Mendoza, 1292

Texas Woman's University v. Chayklintaste, 855, 859

Textile Workers v. Lincoln Mills, 1537

Theodore v. Delaware Valley School District, 1146–1147

Theta Kappa, Inc. v. City of Terre Haute, 1172

Thiel College & Thiel College Chapter, AAUP, 494

Thomas v. Bennett, 851, 1441

Thomas v. Chicago Park District, 1009, 1014

Thomas v. City of Mount Vernon, 357

Thomas v. Davidson Academy, 926n

Thomas v. Granville Board of Education, 1240

Thomas v. Lamar University-Beaumont, 1088

Thomas; United States v., 1393–1394

Thomas Jefferson University v. Shalala, 1399–1400

Thomas M. Cooley Law School v. American Bar Association, 1542, 1546, 1557

Thompson v. City of Los Angeles, 234

Thompson, United States ex rel. v. Columbia/HCA Healthcare, 1401

Tiger Inn v. Edwards, 100

Tilton v. Richardson, 62–63

Time, Inc. v. Firestone, 1108n

Tinker v. Des Moines Independent Community School District, 629, 674, 995–996, 1003, 1053, 1219, 1227, 1240

Tips v. Regents of Texas Tech University, 963

Tipton v. Alexander, 816–817, 853

Tobin v. University of Maine System, 776

Toledo Blade Co., State ex rel. v. University of Toledo Foundation, 1281

Toll v. Moreno, 836

Tolman v. CenCor Career Colleges, Inc., 214

Toney v. Reagan, 558

Torres v. State, 323

Tourville v. Office of Vocational & Educational Services for Individuals With Disabilities, 895

Townsend v. State, 1151

Toyota Motor Manufacturing Kentucky, Inc. v. Williams, 970n

Traficenti v. Morre Catholic High School, 213

Trammel v. United States, 112

Trejo v. Shoben, 551–552, 684–685, 689, 945

Trimble v. Washington State University, 557

Trimble v. West Virginia Board of Directors, Southern West Virginia Community & Technical College, 565–566, 1287

Trister v. University of Mississippi, 687

Troknya v. Cleveland Chiropractic Clinic, 216–217

Troy v. Rutgers, the State University of New Jersey, 499

Trustees of Columbia University v. Columbia/HCA Healthcare Corp., 1365

Trustees of Dartmouth College v. Woodward, 41

Trustees of Rutgers University v. Piscataway Township in Middlesex County, 1191

Trustees of State Colleges & Universities v. NCAA, 1572

Trustees of Tufts College v. City of Medford, 1178

Trustees of Tufts College v. Ramsdell, 851

Trustees of Union College v. Members of the Schenectady City Council, 1178

Tucker v. State of California Department of Education, 611

Tucker v. Watkins, 1253

Tullis v. Pittsburgh State University, 207

Tulsa Area Hospital Council v. Oral Roberts University, 1288

Tuma v. Board of Nursing, 532n

Tunkl v. Regents of University of California, 158–160

Tuomala v. Regent University, 470–471

Turkovich v. Board of Trustees of the University of Illinois, 1622–1623

Tuskegee Institute v. May Refrigeration Co., 185

Tuttle v. Brandeis University, 521–522

U

UAW-Labor Employment & Training Corp. v. Chao, 290

UDC Chairs Chapter, American Association of University Professors v. Board of Trustees of the University of the District of Columbia, 571

Unborn Child Amendment Committee v. Ward, 1289

Unger v. National Residents Matching Program, 579n, 729–730

Unincorporated Operating Division of Indiana Newspapers v. Trustees of Indiana University, 1285

United Carolina Bank v. Board of Regents of Stephen F. Austin State University, 233–234, 237

United Mine Workers v. Gibbs, 96–97

United Mine Workers; United States v., 125

United States v. See name of opposing party

United States Department of Transportation v. Paralyzed Veterans of America, 1478–1479, 1574

United States ex rel. See name of party

United States Fidelity & Guaranty Co. v. Jacksonville State University, 1618

United States Trust Co. v. New Jersey, 272, 477–478

United Steelworkers v. Warrior & Gulf Navigation Co., 36

Uni-United Faculty v. Iowa Public Employment Relations Board, 295

Universal City Studios, Inc. v. Corley, 1354

Universal City Studios, Inc. v. Reimerdes, 1354

Universidad Central de Bayamon v. NLRB, 284

University & Community College System of Nevada v. Farmer, 526–527

University Book Store v. Board of Regents of the University of Wisconsin System, 1364

University Education Association v. Regents of the University of Minnesota, 499

University for Study of Human Goodness & Creative Group Work, In re, 1637

University Hospital, University of Cincinnati College of Medicine v. State Employment Relations Board, 301

University Medical Center Corporation v. The Department of Revenue of the State of Arizona, 245

University of Alabama v. Garrett, 960

University of Alaska v. Geistauts, 704, 1278

University of Alaska v. Modern Construction, Inc., 1598

University of Baltimore v. Peri Iz, 538–539

University of Colorado Foundation v. American Cynamid, 1651–1652

University of Connecticut v. Freedom of Information Commission, 1036, 1283

University of Denver v. Whitlock, 207–208

University of Detroit; EEOC v., 291, 301

University of Dubuque, 494

University of Florida v. KPB, Inc., 1365–1366

University of Great Falls v. NLRB, 285

University of Hawaii Professional Assembly v. Cayetano, 478

University of Houston v. Elthon, 329

University of Illinois; Doe v., 1499, 1500

University of Iowa Hospitals & Clinics v. Shalala, 1400–1401

University of Kentucky v. Courier-Journal, 1283

University of Maryland v. Maas, 225–226

University of Maryland Medical System Corporation; Doe v., 970–971

University of Michigan; Doe v., 1021, 1023

University of Michigan Board of Regents v. Department of Treasury, 1638

University of Minnesota v. Chase, 1280

University of Nevada v. Stacey, 557

University of New Hampshire Chapter AAUP v. Haselton, 287

University of New Haven, 494

University of North Carolina, In re, 1638–1639

University of North Dakota v. Young Men's Christian Association, 154

University of Notre Dame; EEOC v., 701

University of Pennsylvania v. EEOC, 113, 127, 132, 623, 625, 700, 702–703, 705, 1584

University of Pittsburgh, 494

University of Pittsburgh, Appeal of, 1186

University of Pittsburgh v. City of Pittsburgh, Commission on Human Relations, 1161

University of Rhode Island v. University of Rhode Island Chapter of the American Association of University Professors, 298

University of Rochester v. Wagner, 1189–1190

University of San Francisco, 495

University of San Francisco & University of San Francisco Faculty Association, 483

University of Tennessee v. Elliott, 119–120, 240n

University of Texas v. Camenisch, 893–894

University of Texas Medical School v. Than, 917, 986, 1119

University of Vermont & State Agricultural College, 278–279

University of West Virginia Board
of Trustees v. Van Voorhies,
1360, 1651
University Patents, Inc. v.
Kligman, 1360, 1650–1651
University System of Maryland v.
The Baltimore Sun Co.,
1283–1284
University System of New
Hampshire v. United States
Gypsum Co., 1602
University System of New Hamp-
shire Board of Trustees,
Appeal of, 495
Upadhya v. Langenburg, 572
Upjohn Co. v. United States,
109–110
Urbano v. Board of Managers
of New Jersey State Prison,
235–236
Urofsky v. Allen, 659, 1384n
Urofsky v. Gilmore, 622, 625,
626n, 655, 658–665
UWM Post, Inc. v. Board of
Regents of the University of
Wisconsin System, 1022, 1023
Uzzell v. Friday, 1066–1067

V

Vaca v. Sipes, 298
Vacco v. Quill, 1289n
Valentine v. Smith, 523
Vanderbilt v. Colorado Mountain
College District, 650n
Vanderbilt University; Doe v.,
806–807
Vangeli v. Schneider, 881
Vargo v. Hunt, 914
Varma v. Bloustein, 555
Veal v. First American Savings
Bank, 853, 1376
Vega v. Miller, 957
Vermont Agency of Natural
Resources v. United States ex
rel. Stevens, 1405, 1438
Vermont State Colleges Faculty
Federation v. Vermont State
Colleges, 289, 495
Vernonia School District 47J v.
Acton, 1143–1144
Village of. See name of village
Villyard v. Regents of the Univer-
sity System of Georgia,
1623–1624
Virginia v. Black, 869, 995–996,
1020–1021, 1026
Virginia; United States v., 74, 129,
525, 764–767, 783, 1499
Virginia College Building Author-
ity v. Lynn, 66, 1248
Virginia State Board of Pharmacy v.
Virginia Citizens Consumer
Council, 1105–1106, 1229, 1230
Vizcaino v. Microsoft Corporation,
259

Vlandis v. Kline, 826–827, 828, 830
Volt Information Sciences v. Board
of Trustees of Leland Stanford
Junior University, 1597–1598

W

Waffle House; EEOC v., 274
Wagenblast v. Odessa School
District, 158–160
Wagner v. Miskin, 98
Wahba v. New York University, 44
Waldrep v. Texas Employers
Insurance Association, 324
Walgren v. Board of Selectmen of
the Town of Amherst,
1202–1203
Waliga v. Board of Trustees of
Kent State University, 168,
938–941
Walker v. Board of Regents of the
University System of Georgia,
475
Walker v. Phi Beta Sigma
Fraternity, 1095
Walker v. Schwalbe, 351n
Wallace v. Broyles, 1151–1152
Wallace v. Florida A&M Univer-
sity, 913
Walters v. President & Fellows of
Harvard College, 1481
Walz v. Tax Commission of City of
New York, 62, 69
Wang v. Moore, 334
Ward v. Rock Against Racism,
1005, 1014
Ward v. Temple University, 830
Warder v. Board of Regents of the
University of the State of New
York, 1258–1259
Ware; People v., 182
Waring v. Fordham University,
473
Warren County Community Col-
lege v. Warren County Board
of Chosen Freeholders, 172
Wascura v. Carver, 317
Washington v. Central State
University, 263–264
Washington v. Chrisman, 865
Washington v. Glucksberg, 1289
Washington, City of v. Board of
Assessment Appeals of
Washington County, 1196
Washington Federation of State
Employees, AFL-CIO Council
28 v. Spokane Community
College, 1607–1608
Washington Research Foundation
v. Commissioner, 1654
Washington University; Doe v.,
1467
Watchtower Bible & Tract
Society of New York, Inc. v.
Village of Stratton, 1203,
1230, 1237

Watergate West v. District of
Columbia Board of Zoning
Adjustment, 1175–1176
Waters v. Churchill, 606, 608–609,
690, 691, 692, 698, 1243
Waters v. Metropolitan State
University, 944
Waterson v. Cleveland State
University, 1109–1110
Watson v. Board of Regents of the
University of Colorado,
1220–1221
Watson v. Jones, 59n
Watson v. University of Utah Med-
ical Center, 249
Watts v. United States, 869, 870,
1020–1021
Weaver v. University of
Cincinnati, 292
Webb v. Board of Trustees of Ball
State University, 634, 648,
677, 680, 681
Webb v. Student Loan Funding
Corp., 845
Weber v. Kaiser Aluminum Co.,
446, 522–523
Weidemann v. SUNY College at
Cortland, 976
Weinberger v. Salfi, 827
Weiner Merchant, Debtor, In re,
847
Weinstein v. University of Illinois,
123–124
Weinstock v. Columbia University,
505, 537–538
Weise v. Syracuse University, 45
Weismann v. Freeman, 1346
Weist v. State of Kansas, 531
Weitz v. State, 223, 921
Wellner v. Minnesota State Junior
College Board, 550
Wells v. Tennessee Board of
Regents, 531
Welsh v. Boy Scouts of America,
1577
Welsh v. Wisconsin, 865
Welter v. Seton Hall University,
488–489
Wentworth Institute; NLRB v.,
282, 495
Weser v. Glen, 798
Wesley; People v., 877
West v. Atkins, 42
West Caldwell v. Caldwell, 728
Western Pennsylvania Socialist
Workers 1982 Campaign,
1228
Western State University of South-
ern California v. American
Bar Association, 1542, 1546,
1557–1558
Western Waterproofing Co. v.
Lindenwood Colleges, 1602
Weston v. Carolina Research &
Development Foundation,
246–248, 1281

West Virginia ex rel. Darrell V. McGraw v. Burton, 142–143

West Virginia State Board of Education v. Barnette, 653, 742

Whaley v. County of Tuscola, 1290

Whatley v. Clark, 1201

Wheaton College v. Department of Revenue, 1195, 1249

Wheeler v. Miller, 986–987

White v. Board of Regents of the University of Nebraska, 1364

White v. Davis, 623, 1035, 1210–1211

White v. Winona State University, 292–293

Whiting v. Jackson State University, 512

Whitlock v. University of Denver, 1089

Whittingham v. Board of Elections, 1200

Widmar v. Vincent, 58, 738, 996, 998, 1051n, 1069–1073, 1078, 1221, 1223

Wieman v. Updegraff, 618, 620

Wilbur v. University of Vermont, 810

Wilfred Academy v. Southern Association of Colleges & Schools, 1541–1542

Wilkins v. Bentley, 1200

Will v. Michigan Department of State Police, 238

Williams v. Alabama State University, 350

Williams v. Eaton, 1119

Williams v. Howard University, 45n

Williams v. Lindenwood University, 132, 992

Williams v. Salerno, 1201

Williams; State v., 1262

Williams v. Texas Tech University Health Sciences Center, 570–571

Williams v. Trevecca Nazarene College, 1470

Williams v. University of Cincinnati, 1124

Williamson v. Liptzin, 925

Willis v. Dean Witter Reynolds, Inc., 138

Willner v. University of Kansas, 518

Wills v. Brown University, 950, 958

Wilson v. Glenwood Intermountain Properties, Inc., 859–860

Wilton v. Seven Falls Company, 1376n

Wimberly v. Labor & Industrial Commission of Missouri, 327

Winberg v. University of Minnesota, 1258

Winnick v. Manning, 973

Wirin v. Parker, 1210

Wirsing v. Board of Regents of the University of Colorado, 629–630, 648–649

Wisconsin v. Constantineau, 548

Wisconsin v. Mitchell, 1020

Wisconsin v. Yoder, 1266

Witczak v. Gerald, 343

Witters v. Department of Services for the Blind, 841–842

Witters v. State Commission for the Blind, 67

Witters v. Washington Department of Services for the Blind, 63, 67

Wolfe v. Yudichak, 323–324

Wolff v. South Colonie Central School District, 1486

Wolsky v. Medical College of Hampton Roads, 102

Women's Equity Action League v. Bell, 1492

Women's Equity Action League v. Cavazos, 1451, 1492

Wong v. Regents of the University of California, 969–970

Wong-Opasi v. Tennessee State University, 308

Wood v. Davison, 1053

Wood v. Marston, 1278

Wood v. Strickland, 347–348, 924

Woodbridge Terrace Associates v. Lake, 1240–1241

Woodis v. Westark Community College, 915

Woods v. The Wright Institute, 761

Woody v. Burns, 972

Wooley v. Maynard, 653, 742

Woolley v. Hoffmann-La Roche, Inc., 265

Worldwide Volkswagen Corp. v. Woodson, 97

Wounaris v. West Virginia State College, 262–263

Wozniak v. Conry, 645

Wright v. Columbia University, 1140

Wright v. Jeep Corp., 708

Wright v. Schreffler, 878–879

Wright v. Universal Maritime Service Corp., 299

Wurth v. Oklahoma City University, 543

Wygant v. Jackson Board of Education, 512, 796, 824

Wynne v. Loyola University of Chicago, 337

Wynne v. Tufts University School of Medicine, 773, 965–966, 967–968

Wyoming ex rel. Wyoming Agricultural College v. Irvin, 1299

Y

Yacovelli v. Moeser, 624–625, 746n

Yale Club of Chicago v. Department of Revenue, 244

Yale University, 302

Yanow v. Seven Oaks Park, 1171

Yapuncich, In re, 845

Yarcheski v. Reiner, 630n

Yates v. Board of Regents of Lamar University System, 470

Yeagle v. Collegiate Times, 1108–1109

Yellow Springs Exempted Village School District v. Ohio High School Athletic Association, 1129n

Yench v. Stockmar, 973

Yeshiva University v. Greenberg, 1359–1360

Yeshiva University; NLRB v., 491–493

Yesudian ex rel. United States v. Howard University, 1405

YMCA of Philadelphia v. City of Philadelphia, 1197

Young, Ex parte, 235, 1311n

Younger v. Harris, 100n

Younus v. Shabat, 509n

Z

Zablocki v. Redhail, 619

Zahorik v. Cornell University, 108

Zarilla v. Reading Area Community College, 312n

Zavaletta v. American Bar Association, 1548

Zelman v. Simmons-Harris, 841

Zinno v. Patenaude, 329

Zuelsdorf v. University of Alaska, Fairbanks, 544

Zukle v. Regents of the University of California, 962, 968

Zumbrun v. University of Southern California, 730

Zurcher v. Stanford Daily, 1097, 1208, 1245

Subject Index

A

AAAHC (Accreditation Association for Ambulatory Health Care), 893
AACRAO. *See* American Association of Collegiate Registrars and Admissions Officers
AAHE (American Association for Higher Education), 718
AAUP. *See* American Association of University Professors
AAUW (American Association of University Women), 941–42
Abbe, K. H., 1369
Abelson, R., 419
ABOR. *See* Academic Bill of Rights
Abortion, legal issues regarding, 890–892, 1289, 1443–1446
Abstention doctrine, 100
Academic Bill of Rights (ABOR), 746–747, 1018
Academic custom and usage:
    faculty contracts, 479–482, 582–586;
    overview, 35–37, 1582
Academic deference, 8, 80–81, 126–132
Academic freedom:
    Academic Bill of Rights (ABOR), 746–747, 1018;
    administrators' authority over, 693–699;
    basic concepts and distinctions, 613–615;
    claims, methods of analyzing, 648–653;
    in classroom, 628–644;
    confidential information, privilege for, 699–706;
    defamation, defense against, 221;
    external versus internal restraints, 622–625;
    extramural speech, 688–692;
    foundational constitutional law cases, 617–622;
    generally, 605–613;
    governance matters, speech on, 667–683;
    in grading, 644–648;
    "institutional" academic freedom, 625–627, 665–685;
    intramural speech on extramural public affairs, 683–685;
    personnel issues, 700–706;
    in private institutions, 653–654;
    in private life, 685–692;
    professional versus legal concepts, 615–617;
    in publication, 654–665;
    in religious institutions, 714–716;
    in research, 654–665, 706–714;
    of students, 737–747;
    in teaching, 627–654;
    terrorism, war on, effect of, 624;
    Title VII, 702
Academic sanctions. *See* Sanctions
Academic senates, authority of, 187–188

Access to campus. *See* Campus access
Accreditation:
    agencies, 1530–1534, 1559–1560;
    antitrust law, 1546–1549;
    bankruptcy law, 1553–1554;
    case law, 1534–1538;
    common law, 1534–1543;
    constitutional requirements, 1543–1546;
    courts and, 1534–1554;
    defamation law, 1549–1553;
    formative developments, 1534–1538;
    Secretary of Education, role of, 1532–1533, 1534, 1546, 1554, 1559–1560;
    types, 1531;
    U.S. Department of Education, role of, 1554–1559
Accreditation Association for Ambulatory Health Care (AAAHC), 893
ACE. *See* American Council on Education (ACE)
ACHA (American College Health Association), 893
Achtenberg, R., 464, 599
ADA. *See* Americans With Disabilities Act
Adams, J. F., 151, 157, 164
Adams, M., 790
Administrative Conference of the United States, 1521
Administrative procedure laws, 1286–1288

Administrators:
  academic freedom over,
    693–699;
  authority of, 181–187;
  unauthorized acts, 185–186
Admissions:
  affirmative action programs,
    781–803;
  age discrimination, 775–777;
  of aliens, 778–781;
  arbitrariness standard of
    review, 754–755;
  basic legal requirements,
    752–754;
  contract theory, 755–758;
  disability discrimination,
    768–775;
  immigration-status discrimina-
    tion, 778–781;
  learning disabilities, students
    with, 773–775;
  racial discrimination, 758–762;
  readmission, 803–808;
  residency discrimination,
    777–778;
  sex discrimination, 762–768;
  standardized tests, 767
Admission taxes, 1197–1199
ADR. See Alternative dispute
  resolution
Adverse impact claims. See
  Disparate impact claims
Advertising in student press,
  1105–1106
Advisory Commission on Intergov-
  ernmental Relations, 1517
Affiliated organizations. See
  Captive and affiliated
  organizations
Affirmative action:
  in admissions, 781–803;
  conclusions, 455–456;
  equal protection, 449–455;
  Executive Order 11246, 443;
  Executive Order 11375, 443;
  faculty employment decisions,
    522–528;
  federal civil rights statutes,
    1471–1472;
  in financial aid, 820–825;
  overview, 442–445;
  Section 1981, 820–821;
  state regulation of, 455;
  Title VI, 782–783, 786–788,
    795, 1471–1472;
  Title VII, 443–449;
  Title IX, 782–783, 1471–1472
Age discrimination. See also
  Age Discrimination Act; Age
    Discrimination in
    Employment Act:
  in admissions, 775–777;
  in employment, 378–379,
    399–403, 430–433, 516–517;
  older faculty and changes in
    work assignments, 521–522;

retirement incentive packages,
    402, 432–433;
  salary decisions, 517–521;
  termination of employees, 364
Age Discrimination Act:
  administrative enforcement,
    1489, 1490n;
  affirmative action, 1472;
  enforcement remedies,
    1493–1501;
  overview, 1469–1471;
  "program or activity," defined,
    1479–1481;
  retaliatory acts, coverage of,
    1483;
  scope, 1472;
  unintentional discriminatory
    acts, coverage of, 1474–1477
Age Discrimination in Employ-
    ment Act (ADEA):
  collective bargaining, 298;
  disparate impact claims, 401;
  generally, 399–403;
  retaliation claims, 300;
  retirement incentive packages,
    402, 432–433;
  salary discrimination, 517
Agency law and legal
    liability, 91
Age of majority, 726–727
Agthe, D. R., 913n, 1239n
Ahrens, R. Z., 721
Aiken, R., 164
Alcohol use and abuse:
  alcoholics, employment
    discrimination against, 393;
  fraternities and sororities, use
    by, 1088–1090, 1093–1096;
  institutional tort liability for
    injuries related to, 210;
  reporting requirements, 1429
Alexander, K., 1385
Alexander, L., 391
Alger, J. R., 14, 81, 1046
Alienage discrimination. See
  National origin discrimination
Aliens:
  admission of, 778–781;
  documented versus undocu-
    mented status, 833–840;
  employment of, 317–320,
    408–411;
  federal regulation of,
    1314–1318;
  financial aid discrimination,
    833–840;
  visas, 318–319
Alkire, A., 213
Allee, D., 1183
Alston, E. R., 415n
Alternative dispute resolution
    (ADR):
  application to colleges and
    universities, 138–140;
  arbitration, 137–138;
  mediation, 136–137;

overview, 134;
  Title IX, 136;
  types, 135–138
Amaury, N., 20
Ambash, J. W., 1511, 1521
Amendment of employment
    contracts, 271–272
American Association for Higher
    Education (AAHE), 718
American Association for the
    Advancement of Science, 1526
American Association of Colle-
    giate Registrars and Admis-
    sions Officers (AACRAO),
    1048, 1528n
American Association of
    Community Colleges, 1525
American Association of State
    Colleges and Universities,
    1525
American Association of Univer-
    sity Professors (AAUP):
  academic custom and
    usage, 1582;
  academic freedom, 135,
    613–614, 615–617, 628,
    652, 693;
  academic governance, 666;
  conflicts of interest, 1661;
  copyright, 1336, 1345–1346;
  distance education, 1345–1346;
  external regulation of academic
    activities, 1275;
  faculty contracts, 472–473, 482;
  faculty dismissals, 558;
  financial exigency, 579–580,
    583n, 585, 596;
  institutional responsibility for
    legal demands on faculty,
    156;
  Internet address, 1526;
  nonrenewal of contracts, 552;
  overview, 1581–1584;
  part-time faculty, 485;
  post-tenure review, 542;
  publications, 81, 597, 603, 901,
    1589, 1590;
  religious institutions, academic
    freedom in, 715–716;
  sexual harassment, 955;
  student rights, 737–738;
  tenure issues, 531, 572
American Association of
    University Women (AAUW),
    941–942
American College Counseling
    Association, 1528n
American College Health
    Association (ACHA), 893
American College Personnel
    Association, 1528n
American Council on Education
    (ACE), 34, 747, 768, 959n,
    1380, 1525, 1527
American Council on Learned
    Societies, 1526

American Federation of Teachers, 366

American Immigration Lawyers Association, 368

American Institute for Architects, 1611

American Legion and Title IX issues, 1462

Americans With Disabilities Act (ADA):
athletic associations and conferences, 1577–1581;
contingent workers, 260;
drug testing, 269;
employment discrimination, 391–399;
extraterritorial application, 373;
financial aid, 819;
health insurance, 313;
overview, 959–960, 1381–1384, 1468;
reasonable accommodations, 316;
student athletes, 1141

Amusement taxes, 1197–1199

Anderson, E., 164

Anderson, P., 1157

Anderson, R. N., 210n

Anderson, T. H., 466

Andrews, G., 1588

Angell, G. W., 366

Animal and Plant Health Inspection Service, 1325, 1334

Animals:
laws governing using in research, 1325–1329;
patentability of, 1358

Antiterrorism measures, 1334

Antitrust law:
accreditation actions, 1546–1549;
athletic associations and conferences, 1546–1549;
auxiliary enterprises, 1632–1633;
overview, 1368–1375;
research collaboration, 1654–1655

Antonini, T., 890

Applebome, P., 1459

Applegate, J. S., 1379

Arbitration:
collective bargaining, 296–297;
contract cases, 1597–1598;
litigation involving, 138–140;
mandatory, 273–275;
overview, 137–138

Argetsinger, A., 1250

Armstrong, J. R., 1663

Arnsbarger, L. A., 1422, 1654

Aronowitz, S., 19

Arriola, E., 1517

Article I of U.S. Constitution:
chartering of D.C. colleges, 27;

commerce power, 1301–1304;
contracts, state power to modify, 272;
copyright law, basis for, 1334;
patent law, basis for, 1355;
spending power, 1299;
taxing power, 1299

Article III of U.S. Constitution:
federal courts, judicial power of, 1307–1308;
immunity, 231–240

Article IV of U.S. Constitution, 119, 405n

Article VI of U.S. Constitution, 836

Ashenfelter, O., 517

Ashford, D., 1515

Association for Student Judicial Affairs, 1527

Association of Academic Health Centers, 1661

Association of American Colleges and Universities, 737–738, 1528n

Association of American Law Schools, 1336

Association of American Medical Colleges, 1528n, 1658, 1661

Association of American Universities, 1525

Association of Catholic Colleges and Universities, 1528n

Association of College and University Housing Officers—International, 1528n

Association of Community College Trustees, 1528n

Association of Fraternity Advisors, 1528n

Association of Governing Boards of Universities and Colleges, 1155, 1528n

Association of Jesuit Colleges and Universities, 1528n

Assumption of risk, 202–203

Athletic associations and conferences:
ADA, 1577–1581;
antitrust laws, 1566–1571;
common law, 1571–1573;
federal constitutional constraints, 1561–1564;
overview, 1560–1561;
state statutes regulating, 1564–1566;
Title VI, 1574–1577;
Title IX, 1573–1574

Athletic coaches, sex discrimination against, 420–425

Athletics teams and clubs:
disability discrimination, 1140–1142;
drug testing, 1142–1147;
due process rights of athletes, 1115–1119;

Equity in Athletics Disclosure Act, 1123;
freedom of speech for athletes, 1119–1121;
general principles, 1114–1115;
injuries, liability for, 1147–1153;
scholarships, 1123–1127;
sex discrimination, 1127–1140;
statutory law, 1121–1123;
Student-Right-to-Know Act, 1122–1123

Attorney-client privilege, 109–112

Attorneys:
ethical issues, 150;
in-house staff counsel, 143;
services, delivery of, 140–144;
student legal services, 900–901;
treatment law versus preventive law, 144–150

Attorney's fees, 123–125, 510

At-will doctrine of contracts, 262–263

Authority:
of administrators and officers, 181–187;
of campus organizations, 187–188;
question of, 167–171;
sources and scope of, 171–189;
of trustees, 171–181, 188–189

Auxiliary enterprises:
administering, 1639–1640;
antitrust law, 1632–1634;
institutional authority to operate, 1621–1628;
noncompetition statutes, 1628–1632;
overview, 1618–1621;
in private institutions, 1627–1628;
in public institutions, 1621–1627;
taxation of income from entrepreneurial activities, 1634–1639

B

Babbitt, E. M., 220, 587, 603, 1043

Bach, J. L., 1042

Background checks of potential employees, 358–359

Baez, B., 599, 721

Baharlias, A. D., 1508

Bailey, C. M., 1087n

Bakaly, C., 1295

Baker, T. R., 1042

Bakken, G. M., 86

Baldridge, J. V., 496

Baldus, D. C., 463, 599

Bales, R. A., 161

Bandman, M., 1599

Banick, L., 1611

Bankruptcy law:
 accreditation, withdrawal of,
  1553–1554;
 federal student loan programs,
  849–854;
 overview, 842–846;
 school closings, 1376;
 transcripts, withholding of
  from debtors, 846–849
Barbre, E. S., 222n
Barefoot, B. L., 1509
Barmore Zucker, L. S., 882–883
Barnard, T. H., 464, 599
Barnett, S., 1294
Bartlett, J., 1656
Bartow, A., 1508
Basinger, J., 1533
Bateman, M., 905
Bateman, T. A., 190n, 809n
Baxter, F. V., 1518
Bayer, A., 719
Bazluke, F. T., 251
Beach, J. A., 83
Beale, J. R., 163
Bearby, S., 1364
Beauchamp, T. L., 1665
Beckham, J. C., 82, 871, 902, 1292
Beh, H. G., 735, 902, 1508
Bell, D. A., Jr., 904, 1518
Bell, H., 77n
Bell, S., 1509
Bello, C., 333n
Belman, D., 286
Benbow, S., 1509
Bender, K., 75n
Bennett, B., 1509
Berenson, R. A., 1514
Berger, B. J., 324
Berger, C. J., 973, 1045
Berger, V., 973, 1045
Berman, E. M., 276n, 365
Berman, J., 907
Berman, P., 623n, 658n, 746
Bernard, D. J., 270
Berne Convention, 34
Berrian, A. L., 1521
Berry, R. C., 1156
Beshara, D., 718
Bess, J. L., 249
Biagioli, M., 1509
Bickel, R. D., 82, 163, 251, 1114,
 1245
Biedzynski, K. W., 1157
Bienstock, R. E., 1509
Biles, G. E., 598
Bittker, B., 1515
Bjork, L. G., 903
Black, B., 721
Blackwell, J. E., 1521
Blasi, V., 904, 1046
Blechman, R. S., 84
Block, D. J., 163
Bloland, H., 1531, 1586
Blum, D., 494
Blum, G. L., 266n
Blum, K., 346

Blumenstyk, G., 33, 140, 1336,
 1339
Blumrosen, A., 1502
Bodner, G., 492
Bok, D., 18, 83, 1663
Bollag, B., 20, 897, 1069
Bolton, J., 1533
Bombardieri, M., 211
Bompey, S. H., 599
Bond, J., 874
Bookman, M., 254, 900, 1662
Bordone, R. C., 162
Boswell, D. A., 1509
Boswell, L., 1588
Bourdeau, J. A., 1381n
Bowen, H., 483
Bowen, W. G., 902, 1115
Bowie, N. E., 1663
Bowman, C. G., 251
Bowman, J. S., 276n, 365
Boyd, J. P., 108n
Boy Scouts and Title IX
 issues, 1462
Boys Nation and Title IX issues,
 1462
Boys State and Title IX
 issues, 1462
Brademus, J., 1521
Brainard, J., 1377n
Brake, D., 1156, 1157
Bramhall, E. H., 721
Brand, N., 161
Brandenburg, J., 955
Branscomb, A. W., 908
Braxton, J., 719
Breach of contract, 1595–1597
Brennan, W. J., 86
Brevitz, K., 81
Brint, S., 13
Brody, P. M., 1665
Brown, K. W., 231n, 1295
Brown, R. S., Jr., 597, 613, 719,
 1363, 1582
Brown, V. L., 1043, 1079, 1251
Brown, W., 89, 1183
Brown-Scott, W., 1518
Brunner, M. T., 1186n, 1195n
Bryant, J. A., Jr., 412n
Buckman, D. F., 314n, 1402n
Buckner, D. E., 1192n
Bucy, P., 1401
Burdens of proof, 114–118
Bureau of National Affairs, 602
Burgan, M., 623
Burgoyne, R., 110, 160
Burk, D., 1514
Burke, A. M. W., 1405
Burling, P., 164, 252, 367,
 908, 1437
Burns, B. H., 1156
Busey, J. C., 1567
Business/industrial community:
 auxiliary enterprises,
  1618–1628;
 competitor, college as,
  1618–1640;

 contract context for college
  business transactions,
  1591–1598;
 purchaser, college as,
  1599–1618;
 research collaborator, college
  as, 1640–1662;
 seller, college as, 1618–1640
Buss, W. G., 985
Butler, B. B., 905
Butterfield, F., 753
Byman, A., 1509
Byrne, J. P., 613, 665, 717, 718,
 742n, 1046

C

Cabranes, J. A., 181
Cage, M. C., 13, 1261
Calamari, J. D., 580, 1592, 1596
Cameron, C. A., 542
Campbell, A. M., 400n, 433n, 843n
Campbell, B., 41
Campbell, T., 519
Campfire Girls and Title IX issues,
 1462
Campus access:
 commercial solicitation on
  campus, 1230–1236;
 noncommercial solicitation on
  campus, 1236–1239;
 public versus private institutions, 1211–1213;
 speakers and events, exclusion
  of, 1213–1217;
 trespass statutes, 1217–1229
Campus computer networks. *See
 also* Internet:
 freedom of speech, 866–873;
 liability issues, 873–876;
 negligence issues, 198;
 overview, 1384;
 statutes regarding, 1385–1397
Campus Legal Information
 Clearinghouse, 81
Campus Mediation Resources, 161
Campus organizations, administrative authority of, 187–188
Campus security:
 CSA, 885–888;
 CSCPA, 885–888;
 security officers, 876–879;
 violent crime, protecting
  students against, 880–885
Campus Security Act (CSA),
 885–888
Campus Sex Crimes Prevention
 Act (CSCPA), 885–888
Captive and affiliated
 organizations:
 liability issues, 249–250;
 overview, 241–242;
 regulatory laws, 246–248;
 "state action" issues, 248–249;
 structural problems, 242–244;
 taxation issues, 244–246

Carboni, R., 1643
Card, D., 517
Carlson, R. R., 365
Carmichael, M. L., 1291n
Carnegie Council on Policy Studies in Higher Education, 15
Carnegie Foundation for the Advancement of Teaching, 11
Carnevale, D., 782n
Carstensen, P. C., 1589
Carter, S. L., 1509
CAS (Council for the Advancement of Standards in Higher Education), 1527
Catalano, C. G., 990n
Catholic Church, academic freedom and, 714–716
Catlin, E., 1157
CCC (Copyright Clearance Center), 1338
CDC (Centers for Disease Control and Prevention), 1334
Cecil, J. S., 721
Center for Academic Integrity, 916
Center for Information Technology and Privacy Law, 907
Center for Women's Policy Studies, 748
Centers for Disease Control and Prevention (CDC), 1334
Centra, J. A., 599
Chadd, C. M., 1510
Chait, R., 17, 250
Chait, R. P., 597
Chamallas, M., 956
Chamberlain, L., 205
Chamberlin, G. K., 1041n
Chambers, C. M., 1547, 1588
Chamblee, D. A., 1518
Chapman, M., 1572
Chapus, D. P., 213n, 222n
Charles, R., 1514
Charney, S., 1385
Chase, M. P., 1510
Chase, R. F., 1197n
Chastain, G., 1510
CHEA (Council for Higher Education Accreditation), 1531
Cherry, R. L., Jr., 902
Child care services for students, 899–900
Childress, J., 1510
Chin, G., 801
Christman, D. E., 907
Church, T. W., 1047
Civil rights compliance:
    administrative enforcement, 1486–1493;
    affirmative action, 1471–1472;
    Age Discrimination Act. See Age Discrimination Act;
    disability statutes, 1573–1577;
    employment discrimination. See Employment discrimination;
    enforcement remedies, 1493–1501;

extraterritorial acts of discrimination, 1484–1486;
federal enforcement powers, 1304–1307;
general considerations, 1449–1450;
"program or activity," scope of, 1479–1482;
"receiving federal financial assistance," scope of, 1477–1479;
Rehabilitation Act, 1464–1468;
retaliation claims, 1482–1484;
scope and coverage problems, 1472–1486;
spending statutes, 1573–1577;
Title VI. See Title VI;
Title VII. See Title VII;
Title IX. See Title IX;
unintentional discriminatory acts, coverage of, 1474–1477
Civil Rights Restoration Act (CRRA), 1480–1481
Civil service rules, 275–277
Clague, M. W., 602
Claim preclusion, 118–121
Clark, B. R., 83
Clark, M., 464
Clark, R. L., 464
Class action suits, 105–107
Classroom, academic freedom in, 628–644
Claussen, C., 1157
Clemons, J., 367
Cleveland, H., 1295
Closures. See also Reductions in force:
    constitutional considerations, 587–594;
    contractual considerations, 579–587;
    preparing for, 596–597;
    statutory considerations, 594–595
Clother, R. C., 251
Clune, W., III, 1521
Cocurricular activities, liability for injuries related to, 206–210
Cohn, L. M., 392n
Cole, E. K., 464, 599, 902, 956, 1045, 1662
Cole, J. L., 463, 599
Colecchia, T. J., 1510, 1663
Coleman, A. L., 903, 1046
Coleman, B. J., 367
Collective bargaining:
    agency fees, 290–292;
    antidiscrimination laws and, 298–301;
    arbitration, 296–297;
    bargainable subjects, 293–298;
    bargaining unit eligibility, 490–496;
    campus mail systems, use of, 292;
    certification, 287–293;

fact finding, 296;
impasse resolution techniques, 295–297;
interest arbitration, 296;
mediation, 296;
minority unions, 288;
organization, 287–293;
overview, 277–278;
past practices clauses, 497;
at private institutions, 279–282;
at public institutions, 286–287;
public-private dichotomy and, 278;
recognition, 287–293;
at religiously affiliated institutions, 282–286;
rival unions, 288;
by students, 301–303;
Title VII, 298–301;
traditional academic practices, coexistence with, 496–501;
unfair labor practice claims, 297–298;
zipper clauses, 497
College and University Professional Association for Human Resources, 1528n
Colombo, J. D., 1515
Colvin, A. J. S., 161
Commanger, H. S., 737
Commerce Clause:
    athletic conferences, application to, 1565;
    multistate institutions, state regulation of, 1268–1272;
    overview, 1301–1304
Commercial solicitation on campus, 1230–1236
Committee on Foreign Students and Institutional Policy, 13
Committee on Nonprofit Corporations, 1293
Common law:
    accreditation actions, 1534–1543;
    athletic associations and conferences, 1571–1573;
    postsecondary education, law of, 32
Community. See Local governments and local community
Comprehensive Environmental Response, Compensation, and Liability Act (CERCLA) of 1980, 1378–1379
Computers. See Campus computer networks
Condrey, S. E., 366
Conference on Fair Use, 1336
Confidentiality. See Privilege
Conflicts of interest, 150, 1657–1662
Connell, M. A., 164, 420, 437, 540, 1588
Connolly, S. J., 419

Connor, K., 767, 820
Consent decrees, 456
Consortium of College and University Media Centers, 1336
Constitution, U.S. *See* U.S. Constitution; *specific articles and amendments*
Constitutional liability:
  of employees, 346–357;
  of institutions, 230–241;
  issues on the merits, 353–357;
  qualified immunity, 346–353;
  substantive due process, 353–357
Construction contracts:
  general principles, 1610–1612;
  liability problems, 1615–1618;
  in public institutions, 1612–1615
Consumer Product Safety Commission, 1320
Contempt of court, 125–126
Contingent workers, 260
Contracting out. *See* Outsourcing
Contracts:
  academic custom and usage, 479–482, 582–586;
  amendment, 271–272;
  applicants, rights of, 755–758;
  arbitration, 1597–1598;
  at-will doctrine, 262–263;
  breach of contract, 1595–1597;
  collective bargaining, 490–501;
  constitutional due process rights, 547–552;
  construction contracts, 1610–1618;
  defining, 261–262;
  drug testing required by, 267–269;
  elements, 1593–1595;
  employee handbooks as, 265–267;
  employee liability, 344–346;
  executive contracts, 270;
  institutional liability, 225–230;
  interpretation, 263–265;
  legal planning, 273–275;
  mandatory arbitration clauses, 273–275;
  medical screening required by, 269–270;
  nonrenewal, 547–552;
  overview, 469–476, 1591;
  part-time faculty, 482–485;
  promissory estoppel, 345;
  in public institutions, 264–265;
  quasi-contractual claims, 266–267;
  in religious institutions, 485–490;
  remedies for breach, 1595–1597;
  rescission, 267;
  sources, 263;
  statutory rights versus contract rights, 476–479;

students, rights of, 727–737;
  types and terms, 1591–1593;
  waiver of rights, 272–273
Contracts Clause, 272
Convention on the Recognition of Qualifications Concerning Higher Education in the European Region, 34
Conway, M., 1588
Cook, C. E., 1533, 1586
Cooper, C., 599
COPA (Council on Postsecondary Accreditation), 1531
Copeland, J. D., 603
Copyright:
  anticircumvention laws, 1353–1354;
  author's own work, 1339;
  coauthorship, 1346;
  coursepacks, 1337–1338;
  fair use doctrine, 1335–1342;
  generally, 1335–1336;
  guidelines, 1336–1337;
  infringement, liability for, 1346–1350;
  Internet service providers, liability of, 1347–1350;
  licensing, 1350–1351;
  music, 1353;
  overview, 1334–1335;
  peer-to-peer file-sharing technologies, 1340–1341;
  performance rights, 1342–1344;
  research copies, 1338–1339;
  scope of protection, 1352–1353;
  sovereign immunity, 1351–1352;
  standardized tests, 1355;
  term extension, 1354–1355;
  unpublished material, 1339;
  video and other types of expression, 1339–1341;
  "work made for hire" doctrine, 1344–1346
Copyright Clearance Center (CCC), 1338
Copyright Management Center, 1342
Corbally, J., Jr., 163
Council for Higher Education Accreditation (CHEA), 1531
Council for Opportunity in Education, 1528n
Council for the Advancement of Standards in Higher Education (CAS), 893, 1527
Council on Postsecondary Accreditation (COPA), 1531
Coursepacks, fair use of, 1337–1338
Courtade, C. R., 395n, 1465n
Courts:
  abstention doctrine, 100;
  access to, 95–105;
  accreditation actions, 1534–1554;

burdens of proof, 114–118;
  class action suits, 105–107;
  courts of claims, 99;
  deference, academic and judicial, 8, 80–81, 126–132;
  discovery, 107–108;
  evidence, 108–113;
  exhaustion of remedies, 103–105;
  final judgments, 118–121;
  jurisdiction, 95–100;
  litigation management, 132–134;
  mootness doctrine, 101–102;
  motions to dismiss, 113;
  overview, 93–95;
  pretrial and trial issues, 105–121;
  remedies. *See* Remedies;
  standards of judicial review, 114–118;
  standing doctrine, 100–101;
  statutes of limitations, 102–103;
  summary judgments, 113
Cowan, R., 13
Cowen, L., 1245
Cozzillio, M., 1124
Crabb, B. B., 707, 721
Credits. *See* Grades, credits, and degrees
Crego, S., 164
Crews, K. D., 1510
Crime and student protections, 880–885
Criminal prosecutions for student protests, 1010–1012
Crocca, C. A., 1377n
Crockett, R. B., 1292
Croissant, J., 1620
Cropley, A., 14
Cross, K. P., 11, 13
"Cross-cutting" conditions in financial aid programs, 1428–1435
Crow, R. B., 1153n
CRRA (Civil Rights Restoration Act), 1480–1481
CSA (Campus Security Act), 885–888
CSCPA (Campus Sex Crimes Prevention Act), 885–888
Cullen, F. T., 908
Curran, C. E., 719, 721
Curry, J. L., 1510, 1664
Curry, S. J., 1154
Curtner, G., 1655
Customs and Border Protection Bureau, 1315

D

Daane, R. K., 163, 1257, 1277
Daggett, L. M., 1048

Damages:
   capping of, 375n;
   for employment discrimination,
      375n, 382–383;
   overview, 121–122;
   punitive, 383;
   Title VI, 1483;
   Title VII, 121, 387, 1463;
   Title IX, 121
Daniel, P. T. K., 1373
Danne, W. H., Jr., 392n
Dannels, M., 1042
Daugherty, M. S., 250
Davis, C. N., 1295
Davis, D., 83
Davis, M., 1641
Davis, R. J., 289n, 495n
Davis, R. N., 1124
Davis, T., 1005, 1115, 1156,
   1157, 1589
Debt collection:
   federal bankruptcy law,
      842–846;
   student loan programs, 849–854;
   transcripts, withholding of,
      846–849
DeChiara, P., 720, 956
Defamation:
   academic freedom as
      defense, 221;
   by accrediting agencies,
      1549–1553;
   by employees, 337–342;
   institutional liability for,
      217–222;
   privilege as defense, 218–219;
   public figures, 1551–1553;
   in student press, 1108–1114
Defenses:
   assumption of risk, 195,
      202–203;
   sovereign immunity, 192–194,
      1307–1313, 1351–1352,
      1360–1361, 1405
Deference. See Academic defer-
   ence; Judicial deference
De George, R. T., 717, 718
Degrees. See Grades, credits, and
   degrees
Delgado, R., 907
Dell, E., 1655
DelPo, A., 370
De Mitchell, T., 649
Denicola, R. C., 1363
De Palma, A., 514
DeParle, J., 1376
Derrick, J. H., 222n
Design contracts. See
   Construction contracts
DHS. See U.S. Department of
   Homeland Security
Dickerson, J. D., 1572
DiGiovanni, N., Jr., 282, 463, 517,
   598, 599
Digital database providers,
   licensing from, 1350–1351

Dimond, P. R., 1521
DiNardo, L. C., 134, 161
Director, J. J., 298n
Disabilities, persons with:
   discrimination against. See
      Disability discrimination;
   federal statutes, 1381–1384;
   hiring, 357;
   learning disabilities, students
      with, 773–775;
   mental disorders, 427;
   reasonable accommodations,
      316, 391–393, 395–396,
      428–429;
   services for students. See
      Students with disabilities
Disability discrimination. See also
   ADA; Rehabilitation Act:
   in admissions, 768–775;
   in athletics, 1140–1142;
   in employment, 391–399,
      425–430, 515–516;
   federal statutes, 1577–1581
DiScala, J., 927
Disciplinary and grievance
      systems:
   codes of student conduct,
      913–916;
   due process requirements,
      361;
   employee discipline, 360–362;
   establishment of, 911–913;
   judicial systems, 917–921;
   overview, 910–911, 921;
   in private institutions, 924;
   psychiatric illnesses,
      disciplining students with,
      924–927;
   in public institutions, 921–924
Disciplinary sanctions. See
   Sanctions
Discovery, 107–108
Discrimination. See specific types
   of discrimination
Dismissals. See Sanctions
Disner, E. G., 1369
Disparate impact claims:
   ADEA, 401;
   constitutional challenges, 404;
   Equal Pay Act, 385–386;
   sex discrimination, 1135–1136;
   sexual orientation
      discrimination, 441–442;
   Title VI, 1497–1498;
   Title VII, 375–376, 380–381,
      385–386, 388, 401, 404,
      1135–1136, 1474, 1476–1477,
      1497–1498;
   Title IX, 388;
   unintentional discriminatory
      acts, 1474, 1476–1477
Disparate treatment claims:
   pregnancy discrimination, 413;
   Title VII, 375–377, 379–380,
      382, 413
Distance education, 1342–1344

Dixon, R. G., Jr., 904
DOJ. See U.S. Department of
   Justice
DOL. See U.S. Department of
   Labor
Domestic partner benefits,
   439–442
Donaldson, D. M., 1415n, 1416
Donaldson, R. G., 1315n
DOT (U.S. Department of
   Transportation), 1321
Dougherty, F. M., 289n, 395n,
   1465n, 1501n
Douglas, J., 494
Douvanis, G., 905
Downing, T. J., 464, 599
Dressel, P., 1588
Drinan, R. F., 160, 163
Drug-Free Schools and
   Communities Act
   Amendments, 1434–1435
Drug-Free Workplace Act of 1988,
   1432–1434
Drug testing:
   of athletes, 1142–1147;
   of employees, 267–269;
   Fourth Amendment limitations,
      268–269
Drug use and abuse:
   Drug-Free Schools and
      Communities Act
      Amendments, 1434–1435;
   Drug-Free Workplace Act of
      1988, 1432–1434;
   employment discrimination
      against users, 393;
   federal financial aid assistance
      for programs, 1434–1435;
   reporting requirements, 1429;
   in workplace, 1432–1434
Dry, M., 1047
Duckworth, M. B., 325
Duderstadt, J. J., 1115
Due process:
   for athletes, 1115–1119;
   civil rights enforcement
      powers, 1304;
   employee disciplinary actions,
      361;
   nonrenewal of contracts,
      547–552;
   in private institutions,
      571–575;
   procedural, 169, 545,
      547–571, 617–622;
   substantive, 353–357,
      922–924;
   tenure denials, 552–557;
   tenure terminations, 557–567
Duff, J., Jr., 295n
Duffala, D. P., 324n
Dunham, S. S., 163
Duryea, E. D., 22, 1587
Duscha, J., 1155
Dutile, F. N., 987, 1056, 1294
Dziech, B. W., 464, 599

E

Eaton, A. E., 162
Eaton, J., 1533
Eaton, T., 230*n*
Ebbs, S., 16
ED. *See* U.S. Department of
    Education
Educational malpractice,
    institutional liability for,
    213–217
Education associations. *See also*
    specific associations:
    accrediting agencies,
        1530–1560;
    athletic associations and
        conferences, 1560–1581;
    dealing with, 1584–1585;
    legal principles, 1528–1530;
    overview, 1525–1528
Education Commission of the
    States, 1260
EDUCAUSE/Cornell Institute
    for Computer Policy and Law,
    907
Edwards, H. T., 82, 86
EEOC. *See* Equal Employment
    Opportunity Commission
Egerton, J., 1521
Ehrenberg, R. G., 19, 517, 1250
Eisenberg, R. S., 719, 1664
Electronic Privacy Information
    Center, 621*n*
Eleventh Amendment:
    ADEA, 403;
    constitutional liability, 353;
    copyright laws, 1351–1352;
    false claims suits, 1405;
    patent laws, 1361;
    salary discrimination, 384;
    Section 1981 claims, 391;
    Section 1983 claims, 231–240;
    state immunity from federal
        law, 1307–1313;
    waiver of immunity, 97, 234*n*
Elias, S., 1510, 1511
Emotional distress, infliction of:
    by employees, 343;
    institutional liability for, 224;
    NLRA, 293
Employee handbooks as
    employment contracts,
    265–267
Employee performance. *See*
    Performance management
Employee protections:
    ERISA, 311–313;
    FLSA, 305–311, 328;
    FMLA, 313–317, 428, 1306;
    immigration laws, 317–320;
    OSHA, 303–305, 328;
    unemployment compensation
        laws, 325–327;
    USERRA, 330–332;
    whistleblower protections,
        327–330, 1274*n*, 1329, 1437;

workers' compensation laws,
    320–325
Employee Retirement Income
    Security Act (ERISA), 311–313
Employees:
    background checks, 358–359;
    civil service rules, 275–277;
    collective bargaining. *See*
        Collective bargaining;
    constitutional liability, 346–357;
    contract liability, 344–346;
    contracts. *See* Contracts;
    defamation by, 337–342;
    disciplinary actions, 360–362;
    emotional distress, infliction
        of by, 343;
    employment relationships,
        defining, 258–261;
    evaluations, 359–360;
    independent contractors,
        distinguished from, 258–260;
    interference by, 342–343;
    invasion of privacy by, 342;
    leased, 260;
    liability, 332–357;
    negligence, 334–337;
    negligent hiring, supervision,
        or retention, 222–224;
    noncitizens, 317–320;
    overview, 255–258;
    performance improvement
        plans, 360;
    performance management,
        357–364;
    personal liability, 332–357;
    pre-hire issues, 357–359;
    promotions, 362–363;
    protections, 303–332;
    telecommuters, 261;
    termination. *See* Termination
        of employment;
    tort liability, 332–334
Employment discrimination:
    affirmative action. *See*
        Affirmative action;
    age discrimination. *See* Age
        discrimination;
    against alcoholics, 393;
    against athletics coaches,
        420–425;
    "bona fide occupational qualifi-
        cation" exception, 374;
    constitutional prohibitions,
        403–405;
    damages, 375*n*, 382–383;
    disability discrimination.
        See Disability discrimination;
    disparate impact claims.
        See Disparate impact claims;
    disparate treatment claims.
        See Disparate treatment
        claims;
    against drug abusers, 393;
    Equal Pay Act, 383–386;
    Executive Order 11246,
        405–406;

Executive Order 11375,
    405–406;
executive orders, 405–406;
federal civil rights statutes,
    1472–1474;
health benefits discrimination,
    412–414;
interplay of statutes,
    regulations, and constitutional
    protections, 371–373;
judicial deference, 501–510;
national origin discrimination,
    390, 408–411, 510–513;
overview, 501;
pregnancy discrimination,
    412–414;
protected classes, 406–442;
racial discrimination, 389–391,
    406–408, 510–513;
Rehabilitation Act, 391–399;
religious discrimination,
    433–435;
by religious institutions,
    456–462;
remedies, 382–383, 501–510;
retaliation claims, 373;
Section 1981. *See* Section 1981;
Section 1983. *See* Section 1983;
sex discrimination, 386–389,
    411–425, 513–515;
sexual harassment, 414–420;
sexual orientation
    discrimination, 435–442;
sources of law, 374–406;
tenure denial, 501–510;
timely filing requirements,
    381–382;
Title VI. *See* Title VI;
Title VII. *See* Title VII;
Title IX. *See* Title IX
Ende, H., 164
Engle, K., 464
English, F. M., 1191*n*
English-only laws, 409–410
Entrepreneurial activities,
    taxation of income from,
    1634–1639
Environmental laws, 1376–1381
Environmental Protection Agency
    (EPA), 305, 1321, 1377,
    1380–1381
Epstein, E. S., 160
Epstein, M. A., 163
Equal Employment Opportunity
    Commission (EEOC):
    age discrimination, 400, 401;
    contingent workers, 260;
    disability discrimination,
        393–394, 516;
    employment discrimination,
        106*n*, 374–375;
    English-only laws, 409–410;
    mandatory arbitration, 275;
    pregnancy discrimination, 412;
    religious practices, reasonable
        accommodation of, 434;

Equal Employment (*Continued*)
salary discrimination, 385;
sex discrimination, 421–422;
sexual harassment, 414, 420;
workers' compensation, 325
Equal Pay Act, 383–386, 421–424
Equal protection:
affirmative action, 449–455;
civil rights enforcement
powers, 1304;
racial discrimination,
1451–1452;
Section 1983 claims, 1464
Equity in Athletics Disclosure Act,
1123
ERISA. *See* Employee Retirement
Income Security Act
Establishment clause:
government funds, use of in
religious institutions, 61–71;
public institutions, religious
autonomy rights in, 71–75
Estoppel doctrine and unautho-
rized acts of administrators,
185–186
Ethical issues for attorneys, 150,
1657–1662
Euben, D. R., 315, 368, 519,
625, 746*n*
Eurich, N., 14
Evans, E. M., 250
Evans, G. R., 87
Evans, R. B., 19, 252
Evans, T. S., 425
Evans, W. D., Jr., 250
Evidence, 108–113
Exchange visitor program, 1316
Executive contracts, 270
Executive Orders:
11246, 405–406, 443;
11375, 405–406, 443;
12250, 1489;
12549, 1438;
12866, 1505, 1507;
12958, 1507
Exhaustion of remedies, 103–105
External governance, 25–29
Extraterritorial acts of discrimina-
tion, covered by federal civil
rights statutes, 1484–1486

F

Fact finding and collective
bargaining, 296
Faculty:
community activities of,
1239–1244;
contracts. *See* Contracts;
freedom of speech. *See*
Academic freedom;
part-time faculty, 482–485;
private lives, 685–693
Faculty employment decisions:
affirmative action, 522–528;
challenges to, 510–517;

closures, mergers, and
reductions in force, 579–597;
judicial deference, 501–510;
miscellaneous issues, 567–571;
nonrenewal of contracts,
547–552;
overview, 501;
post-tenure review, 542–544;
private institutions, 571–575;
procedures, 544–547;
public institutions,
constitutional due process in,
547–571;
salary decisions, challenges to,
517–521;
standards and criteria, 528–544;
tenure denials, 536–542,
552–557;
tenure terminations, 531–536,
557–567
Fahleson, M. A., 263
Fairchild, J., 194*n*
Fair Labor Standards Act (FLSA):
overview, 305–311;
retaliation claims, 311, 328
Fair use doctrine, 1335–1342
Fairweather, J. S., 1664
False Claims Act, 328, 1404–1406,
1436–1438
Family and Medical Leave
Act (FMLA), 313–317,
428, 1306
Family Educational Rights and
Privacy Act (FERPA):
admissions records, 753;
certified transcripts, withholding from student debtors, 848;
computerized records, 867*n*;
consent requirements, 108*n*;
financial aid records, 812;
health records, 1402–1403;
international students'
records, 899;
overview, 1029–1034;
private causes of action, 1487;
sex offender records, 888;
state open records laws,
1035–1040, 1283–1285;
suicide threats, 212
Fanning, R. W., 368
Fantel, J. I., 536, 603
Farnsworth, E. A., 87
Farrell, E. F., 1069, 1202
Farrington, D. J., 87
Faulkner, F., 938
Faulkner, J. E., 1043
FBI (Federal Bureau of
Investigation), 1332
FDA. *See* Food and Drug
Administration
Federal Bureau of Investigation
(FBI), 1332
Federal Family Educational Loans
(FFEL), 814, 850–851
Federal Mediation and
Conciliation Service, 296

Federal Trade Commission Act,
1375–1376
Federal Unemployment Tax Act
(FUTA), 325–326, 1406, 1414,
1421
Feliu, A. G., 252
Feller, D., 497
Feller, I., 1292
Ferdico, J. N., 1245
Ferguson, R., 206
FERPA. *See* Family Educational
Rights and Privacy Act
FFEL. *See* Federal Family Educational Loans
Fields, K. A., 1665
Fifteenth Amendment, 1307, 1309
Fifth Amendment, 61
Fighting words, 1019, 1023, 1026,
1028, 1121*n*
Final judgments, 118–121
Financial aid:
affirmative action, 820–825;
aliens, discrimination against,
833–840;
athletic scholarships,
1123–1127;
bankruptcy law, 842–846;
college savings plans, 811–812;
"cross-cutting" aid conditions,
1428–1435;
documented aliens,
discrimination against,
833–837;
enforcing compliance,
1435–1438;
federal aid versus federal
procurement, 1424–1425;
federal programs, 812–817;
funding agencies, disputes
with, 1438–1449;
general principles, 808–812;
history, 1423–1424;
legal structure of, 1425–1428;
nondiscrimination principles,
817–820;
nonresidents, discrimination
against, 825–833;
race-exclusive scholarships,
823–825;
"receiving federal financial
assistance," scope of phrase,
1477–1479;
religious institutions, use
of government funds at,
840–842;
student debts, collection of,
842–846;
Title VI, 820, 822, 823, 825;
Title IX, 817–818, 820, 822,
825*n*;
transcripts, withholding of
as debt collection tool,
849–854;
undocumented aliens,
discrimination against,
837–840

Financial exigency. *See* Reductions in force
Fincher, R. D., 162
Finkelstein, M. J., 84
Finkin, M. W., 17, 84, 366, 492, 497, 517, 597, 603, 667, 719, 720, 722, 1246, 1582, 1586, 1587
FIRE. *See* Foundation for Individual Rights in Education
First Amendment:
  academic freedom, 613–614, 617–622, 627, 648–653, 666, 688;
  for athletes, 1119–1121;
  campus computer networks, 866–873, 1389–1393;
  canvassers, rights of, 1203–1205;
  collective bargaining, 282–287, 290–292;
  commercial speech, 1230–1236;
  community access to campus, 1212–1213, 1217–1229;
  community activities of faculty members and students, 1239–1244;
  compelled speech, 1430–1431;
  English-only laws, 409–410;
  events, exclusion of, 1213–1217;
  extramural speech, 688–692;
  faculty contracts in religious institutions, 485–490;
  faculty freedom of expression, 605–613;
  faculty terminations, 588;
  fighting words, 1019, 1023, 1026, 1028, 1121*n*;
  free speech zones, 1005–1006;
  governance matters, speech on, 667–683;
  hate speech, 1017–1029;
  intramural speech on extramural public affairs, 683–685;
  multistate institutions and programs, state regulation of, 1270–1272;
  noncommercial solicitation speech, 1236–1239;
  opinion privilege, 219;
  personnel decisions, 529;
  police surveillance, 1210–1211;
  "public forum" concept, 996–1001, 1390*n*;
  religious institutions, 61, 714–716, 1264–1266;
  religious neutrality, 57–58;
  research findings, protection of, 711–713;
  retaliation claims, 422–423, 588;
  sexual harassment cases, 944–945;
  soliciting and canvassing on campus, 1229–1230;

  speakers, exclusion of, 1213–1217;
  speech codes, 1017–1029;
  student organizations, 1050–1078;
  student press, 1096–1114;
  student protests, 993–1017;
  for students, 993–1029;
  symbolic speech, 995;
  threats, communication of, 1395–1397;
  viewpoint neutrality, 1238*n*
Fischer, P. A., 412*n*
Fischer, T., 1155
Fish, S., 747
Fishbein, E. A., 84
Fisher, B. S., 908
Fishman, J. J., 250
Fishman, P., 1295
Fisk, R. S., 1587
Fiss, O., 907
Fitzgerald, L. F., 600
Fitzgibbon, S. A., 300
Fleming, T. M., 1291*n*
FLSA. *See* Fair Labor Standards Act
Flygare, T. J., 315, 368, 1044, 1511
FMLA. *See* Family and Medical Leave Act
Foerstel, H. N., 1521
Foerster, A., 301
Fogg, P., 540
Folger, J., 82
Food and Drug Administration (FDA), 1319–1324, 1659
Ford, A. T., 597
Ford, D. L., 1045
Foreigners. *See* Aliens
Fossey, R., 649, 885, 905, 909, 1519
Foster, A. L., 1285
Foster, D., 1655
Foster, S., 466, 602
Foster, W. F., 71*n*
Foundation for Individual Rights in Education (FIRE), 916, 1017
Fourteenth Amendment:
  academic freedom, 617–618, 688;
  civil rights enforcement, 1304–1307;
  community access to campus, 1220–1222;
  constitutional liability, 353–357;
  due process. *See* Due process;
  employment discrimination, 403–405;
  equal protection. *See* Equal protection;
  faculty terminations, 588–591;
  minimum contacts clause, 97–98;

  multistate institutions and programs, state regulation of, 1270–1272;
  personnel decisions, 529, 530;
  racial discrimination, 1451–1452;
  religious autonomy in religious institutions, 61;
  Section 1983 claims, 1464;
  state immunity from federal civil rights claims, 1309, 1311;
  student organizations, 1065–1069;
  unwanted medical treatment, right to refuse, 1289
Fourth Amendment:
  athletes, drug testing of, 1142–1147;
  drug testing, limitations on, 268–269;
  local police authority, 1207–1208;
  medical screening, limitations on, 269–270;
  student housing, searches and seizures in, 861–866;
  student press, 1097;
  teaching and research materials, protection for, 612–613
Fowler, D. R., 1664
Francis, L. P., 1044
Frank, R., 1515
Franke, A. H., 135, 162, 212, 213, 362, 462
Franklyn, D. J., 1513
Fraternities and sororities:
  alcohol-related issues, 1088–1090, 1093–1096;
  hazing, 1084–1095;
  houses, tax treatment of, 1188–1191;
  institutional liability, 1087–1093;
  institutional recognition and regulation, 1079–1087;
  liability of, 1093–1096;
  overview, 1078–1079
Fraud, federal regulation of, 1404–1406
Freedom of press. *See* First Amendment
Freedom of religion. *See* First Amendment
Freedom of speech. *See* First Amendment
Free exercise clause, 59–61
Free speech zones, 1005–1006
Freitag, C. N., 1416
Freitas, M., 1156
Frey, J. C., 250
Friedman, R. I., 222*n*
Friendly, H., 41
Fritz, T. P., 365
Frug, J., 1244
Full Faith and Credit Clause, 119
Furniss, W. T., 597, 1590

Fusco, T., 411n
FUTA. See Federal Unemployment
    Tax Act

G

Gaal, J., 425
Gaffney, E. M., 88, 252,
    1294, 1507
Galanter, M., 95
Gallin, A., 84
Gamber, C., 89
Gamble, B. S., 600
Gappa, J. M., 483, 598
Garbarino, J. W., 1584
Garcia, M., 20
Garry, P., 1391n
Gasaway, L. N., 1511
Gay rights. See Homosexuals
Geevarghese, S., 247
Gehring, D. D., 252, 902,
    907, 1518
Geller, R., 1509
General Agreement on Trade in
    Services (GATS), 34
George, B. G., 1589
Geraci, C. P., 252
Getman, J., 719
Ghent, J. F., 407n, 854n, 1128n,
    1167n, 1214n, 1218n
Gifis, S., 87
Giles, M., 909
Gill, J., 87
Gillespie, J. F., 282n
Gindin, S. E., 1511
Ginsberg, W. R., 1244
Girl Scouts and Title IX
    issues, 1462
Girls Nation and Title IX
    issues, 1462
Girls State and Title IX
    issues, 1462
Gitlin, T., 717
Glazer, N., 717
Glazier, M. S., 425
Goldberg, C., 514
Goldberg, D., 1511
Goldblatt, S. M., 1662
Goldman, A. L., 735
Goldoftas, L., 1511
Goldstein, P., 900, 1662
Goode, E., 924
Gooden, N. A., 84
Goodman, R. M., 1406n, 1408,
    1422, 1634n, 1652n, 1654
Goods, purchases of, 1599–1603
Gordon, J., III, 714, 715
Gordon, M. L., 1664
Gose, B., 21
Gouldner, H., 82
Government employees and civil
    service, 275–277
Grades, credits, and degrees:
    academic freedom and,
    644–648;
    awarding of, 927–938;

degree revocation, 938–941;
    overview, 927;
    sexual harassment complaints
    and, 941–959;
    students with disabilities,
    evaluation of, 959
Graduate teaching assistants and
    collective bargaining, 301–303
Gravois, J., 483
Gray, M., 1157
Green, R. M., 252
Greenawalt, R. K., 904
Greer, D. G., 1295
Gregory, B., 1567
Gregory, D. E., 908, 1154
Gregory, D. L., 252, 313, 366
Gregory, J. D., 599
Grey, T. C., 1023, 1047
Grier, M. W., 137
Grievances. See Disciplinary and
    grievance systems
Gross, A. J., 365
Grossman, J., 1295
Grossman, P., 463
Groves, A. W., 904
Guaranteed Student Loans (GSL).
    See Federal Family Educa-
    tional Loans
Guarino, G. A., 303n
Guerin, L., 370
Gulbis, V. M., 1180n
Gulland, E. D., 1084, 1087
Gumport, P. J., 367
Gunderson, M., 286
Gurdus, J., 324
Gutek, B., 600
Gutierrez, P. T., 1406n, 1634n,
    1652n
Guttag, E. W., 1652

H

Haddon, P. A., 719
Hajian, T., 1511, 1521
Hall, J. T., 206
Hall, J. W., 151, 157, 164, 1588
Hall, T. M., 410n
Hamilton, D., 895
Hamilton, J., 20
Hamilton, N., 615, 616, 617,
    666n, 717, 718
Hammond, P. B., 464
Hardin, P., 366
Harding, B. M., Jr., 1408,
    1515, 1516
Harper, G. K., 1334n, 1339, 1342,
    1355n, 1511, 1650n
Harpool, D., 250
Harrington, P. J., 1512, 1664
Harris, J., 1588
Harris, R. G., 1588
Harrison, D. B., 809n, 1291n
Harrison, D. L., 1331, 1386n
Hartley, R., 291n, 1508
Hartman, J. L., 908
Harvard Civil Rights Project, 792

Hassman, P. E., 406n, 809n,
    1171n, 1273n
Hasson, J., 1654
Hasty, K. N., 325
Hate speech:
    case law, 1019–1026;
    guidelines for dealing with,
    1026–1029;
    overview, 1017–1019
Hauser, G. F., 1154
Hawke, C., 867n, 876
Hawkings, M. W., 464
Hawkins, H., 1586
Hawkins, M. W., 599
Haworth, K., 861, 887
Hawthorne, E., 14
Hayden, G. M., 303
Hazard, G., Jr., 144
Hazing by fraternities and
    sororities, 1084–1095
Health Education Assistance
    Loans (HEAL), 850
Health insurance:
    discrimination, 412–414;
    regulation of, 1397–1404
Health Insurance Portability and
    Accountability Act (HIPAA),
    1401–1404
Health Professions Student Loans,
    850
Health services for students,
    888–893
Hebel, S., 746, 747, 1250, 1460n
Heilbron, L. H., 1587
Heisman, L. J., 849n
Heller, D. E., 1293
Heller, G., 1589
Helms, L. B., 82, 84
Hendrickson, R., 1480
Henkin, L. J., 904, 938n
Herman, J., 1046
Hernandez, W., 1066n, 1153
Heumann, M., 1047
HEW (U.S. Department of
    Health, Education and
    Welfare), 1130
Heydrich, M. W., 34
HHS. See U.S. Department
    of Health and Human Services
Hiers, R., 626, 627, 665, 690
Higgins, B., 342
Higgins, J. E., Jr., 366
Hill, F. R., 1408n
Hillman, B., 301
Hines, E. R., 1293
HIPAA, Health Insurance Portabil-
    ity and Accountability Act
Hippensteele, S., 955
Hobbs, W. C., 82
Hodges, M., 873
Hofstadter, R., 625, 737
Hoke, J. R., 846, 905
Hold-harmless agreements,
    153–156
Holland, T. P., 250
Hollander, P., 164

Hollis, J. M., 906
Holloway, W., 365
Holmes, G. W., 901
Homosexuals:
 domestic partner benefits,
  439–442;
 employment benefits for
  partners, 439–442;
 military ban on, 442;
 same-sex harassment, 437–438
Honan, W. H., 17, 1372
Hoofnagle, C., 649, 717
Hoover, E., 211, 303, 775, 1024n,
  1080, 1202, 1283
Hoover, N. C., 1153
HOPE Scholarship Credit, 1415
Hopkins, B., 1295, 1516
Horger, K., 1400
Hornby, D. B., 249
Horowitz, D., 717, 746, 747
Horowitz, H. W., 1293
Horowitz, I. L., 717, 1589
Horton, N. S., 1080
Houle, C. O., 250
Houpt, C., 587
Hovenkamp, H., 1512
Hovey, R., 206
Hoye, W. P., 201, 206, 252
Hoyt, J. W., 28n
Hugel, P. S., 1045
Hughes, E., 1294
Human subjects, laws governing
  use of in research, 1318–1325
Hunnicutt, K., 1017
Hunter, R. J., 368
Hurd, R., 301
Hurley, B., 903, 909
Hursh, R. D., 160n
Hustoles, T. P., 464, 530,
  598, 599
Hutchens, M. B., 366
Hutcheson, P. A., 1590
Hutchins, N. H., 366
Hyatt, D., 286
Hylden, T., 1588
Hynes, J. D., 160

I

IACUC (Institutional Animal Care
  and Use Committees),
  1325–1327
IMMACT. See Immigration Act
  of 1990
Immigration:
 admissions and, 778–781;
 employees and, 317–320;
 federal regulation of, 1314–1318
Immigration Act of 1990
  (IMMACT), 319
Immigration and Customs
  Enforcement, 1314–1315
Immigration Reform and Control
  Act (IRCA) of 1986, 318
Immunity:
 charitable, 194–195;

copyright laws, 1351–1352;
 Eleventh Amendment,
  231–240;
 false claim suits, 1405;
 patent laws, 1360–1361;
 qualified, 346–353;
 sovereign, 192–194;
 state immunity from federal
  law, 1307–1313;
 waiver of, 97, 234n
Indemnification agreements,
  153–156
Independent contractors distin-
  guished from employees,
  258–260, 1604
Industrial community. See
  Business/industrial community
Information, obtaining from fed-
  eral government, 1506–1507
Ingelhart, L. E., 1155
Ingram, R. T., 250
Injunctions, 122–123, 1010–1012
In loco parentis doctrine, 196–197
Institute of Laboratory Animal
  Resources, 1327
Institute of Medicine, 1526
Institutional Animal Care and Use
  Committees (IACUC),
  1325–1327
Institutional constitutional rights
  liability, 230–241
Institutional contract liability,
  225–230
Institutional review boards,
  1319–1324
Interest arbitration, 296
Interference by employees,
  342–343
Internal governance, 24–25
Internal Revenue Service
  (IRS), 1407, 1411–1412,
  1420–1423
International Development Coop-
  eration Agency, 1320
International students:
 services for, 896–899;
 visa requirements, 1314–1318
Internet. See also Campus:
  computer networks;
 freedom of speech, 866–873;
 jurisdiction issues, 98;
 liability issues, 873–876;
 service providers, copyright
  liability of, 1347–1350;
 trademark issues, 1366–1367
Invasion of privacy:
 by employees, 342;
 institutional liability for, 224
IRCA (Immigration Reform and
  Control Act of 1986), 318
IRS. See Internal Revenue Service

J

Jackson, J., 614
Jacobson, J. S., 420, 908

Jacoby, S. B., 1522
Jaffree, N. A., 420
Jameson, J. K., 1042
Jannarone, A., 876
Janosik, S. M., 908
Jasanoff, S., 721
Jaschik, S., 1461
Javanovic, T. B., 400n
Jennings, B. M., 905
Jennings, E. K., 1045
Jewett, C. L., 463, 1519
Joffe, P., 212
Johnson, A. B., 604
Johnson, A. M., Jr., 903
Johnson, L. T., 463
Johnson, W. B., 1184n, 1274n,
  1378n
Johnson, W. T., Jr., 252
Johnston, R. G., 1044
Jones, C. J., 1141, 1157
Jones, D. K., 1516
Jones, N., 1295
Judge, J., 425
Judicial deference:
 faculty employment decisions;
  501–510;
 overview, 8, 80–81, 126–132
Judicial systems for student
  discipline, 917–921
Juergensmeyer, J. C., 1244
Julius, D. J., 367
June, A. W., 1170
Jung, S., 1294
Jurisdiction:
 abstention doctrine, 100;
 Internet, issues relating to
  use of, 98;
 overview, 95–100;
 public institutions, suits
  against, 99
Justiz, M. J., 903

K

Kadue, D. D., 463, 465, 601
Kahin, B., 1357
Kahn, K., 282
Kalaidjian, E., 1245
Kamai, E., 542
Kane, M. J., 1157
Kane, M. K., 161
Kanter, A., 1484
Kaplan, R. L., 1516
Kaplin, W. A., 26n, 82, 84, 88,
  145n, 627, 762n, 869n, 907,
  923, 953, 997n, 1017n, 1041,
  1047, 1129n, 1294, 1508,
  1529n, 1536n, 1587
Kappel, B., 1378
Kapusta, T. J., 392n
Karabel, J., 13
Karnezis, K. C., 305n
Karst, K. L., 1327
Kasunic, R., 1338
Katerberg, R. J., 1324
Katsh, M. E., 874, 908, 1514

Katz, K., 717
Kaufman, H. E., 1468, 1512
Kay, D., 1183
Kaye, R. E., 965n
Keane, A., 1384n
Kearns, E. C., 368
Keefe, J. H., 162
Keeton, M. T., 14
Keeton, W. P., 253
Keith, J. L., 624, 1332, 1334
Kelch, T. G., 1512
Keller, E., 956
Keller, J. J., 368
Kellogg, A. P., 400n
Kells, H. R., 1588
Kelly, E. P., Jr., 366
Kelly, K., 14
Kelly, M., 1516
Kemerer, F., 496
Kempner, D., 900, 1662
Kennedy, R., 903
Kenney, M., 1640, 1642, 1643, 1658
Kepley, D. E., 1408
Kerr, C., 84, 85
Kertz, C., 1654
Kesselman, M. L., 600
Khatcheressian, L. W., 1315
Kibler, W. L., 1044, 1045
King, H. M., 251
King, J. E., 905
King, K., 365
King, R. D., 902
King, R. F., 1520
Kinney, E. D., 1514
Kinser, K., 1559
Kirby, W. T., 1512
Kirk, R., 1266
Kirklin, J., 230n
Kirkwood, J. F., 1517
Kirsch, L., 1380
Kirschten, B. L., 1408n, 1416
Klein, A. S., 810n
Klein, D. A., 973n
Kliever, L. D., 719
Knapper, C., 14
Knight, J., 1583
Kobasic, D. M., 882
Kobylak, W., 411n, 413n
Korpela, A. E., 160n, 190n, 192n, 194n, 222n
Koster, P., 1400
Kramer, D. T., 389n, 407n, 444n, 1097n, 1199n
Krattenmaker, T. G., 908
Kreiser, R. R., 1665
Krejsa, D., 1243
Kris, M. E., 1380
Kruk, T. L., 217n
Kuhns, E., 1559n
Kumin, L. A., 213
Kurland, J. E., 597, 613, 717, 719, 1583
Kurzweil, M., 902

Kushner, M. G., 369
Kussman, P. C., 326n

L

Labor standards, regulation of, 305-311
Lacovara, P., 1441, 1517
Ladenson, R., 717
Ladimer, I., 162, 598
Lake, P. F., 212, 251, 253, 335, 1114
Lam, M., 1656
LaManque, A. S., 87
Landis, D. T., 306n
Landrum, R. E., 1510
Land use. See Zoning and land use regulation
Langford, L., 75n
LaNoue, G., 502, 513, 515, 600
Lape, L. G., 1512
Larose, C. J., 1333
Larsen, S., 210n
Larson, A., 324
LaTourette, A. W., 902
Lattinville, R., 1362
Lawler, J. D., 296n
Lawrence, C. R., III, 1047
Laycock, D., 719, 722
Lazarus, R. J., 1512
Leaffer, M., 1645
League for Innovation in the Community College, 1525
Leased employees, 260
Leatherman, C., 17, 1533
Ledbetter, B. E., 1588
Lee, B. A., 367, 425n, 502, 513, 515, 516, 600, 703, 1480
Leech, M., 365
Legal services. See Attorneys
Leiser, B., 718
Lemley, M., 1514
Lemons, S., 1149n
Leonard, J., 128, 903, 1044
Leskovac, H., 1641, 1657, 1665
Leslie, D. W., 483, 598
Lessig, L., 873, 908
Leveraging Educational Assistance Partnership Program, 814
Levi, J. H., 1516
Levin, S. A., 1115
Levine, A., 85
Levine, R. J., 1512
Lewis, D. M. H., 1154
Lewis, H., Jr., 87
Lewis, L., 717
Liability. See also Risk: management;
agency law, 91;
avoiding, 93;
captive and affiliated organizations, acts of, 249-250;
constitutional liability. See Constitutional liability;

contract liability, 344-346;
copyright infringement, 1346-1350;
of employees, 332-344;
enforcement mechanisms, 92-93;
overview, 90-91;
personal, 188-189;
remedies for violations, 93;
tort liability. See Tort liability of trustees, 188-189;
types, 91
Liability insurance, 152-153
Libel. See Defamation
Licata, C., 544
Licensing from digital database providers, 1350-1351
Lifetime Learning Credit, 1415
Light, P., 366
Light, R. J., 903
Light, S. A., 1520
Lindemann, B. T., 463, 465, 601
Linden, D. A., 477n
Linehan, P. F., 1376
Linnell, R. H., 1658
Lipinski, T., 1332, 1386n
Lipka, S., 1069
Lipp, M., 251
Lipset, S. M., 717
Lipsky, D. B., 162
Lisman, N., 1521
Litigation. See Courts
Lobbying, restrictions on federal funds for, 1427-1428
Local governments and local community:
community access to campus, 1211-1239;
community activities of faculty members and students, 1239-1244;
general principles, 1161-1166;
land use regulation, 1167-1183;
police, institutional relations with, 1206-1211;
solicitating and canvassing on campus, 1229-1239;
student voting in the community, 1199-1206;
taxation, 1183-1199;
trespass statutes, 1217-1229;
zoning, 1167-1183
Lockhart, J., 402n, 1465n
Loewe, E. Y., 903
Loewy, A., 903
Long, N. T., 163
Loomis, F., 1480
Lopez, D. E., 713
Loundy, D. J., 1512
Lovain, T., 531
Lowell, C. H., 1157
Lowery, J. W., 916
Ludolph, R. C., 604

Lukianoff, G., 1023
Lund, J., 286, 367

M

MacLachlan, J., 1154
Madsen, H. H., 1296
Magner, D. K., 17, 19
Majestic, M., 1509
Makar, S. D., 733
Malin, M., 717
Mallon, W. T., 470
Malpert, R. A., 369
Manas, A. E., 1366
Mandatory retirement, 399–400, 430, 516–517
Mangan, K. S., 174, 760, 1017, 1534
Manley, A., 194n
Manley, F. B., 140
Mann, R. J., 1358
Mansfield, C., 1376
Manthei, J. R., 324
Maranto, C. L., 286, 367
Marcotte, P., 1379
Marcus, E. H., 416
Marmur, S., 1129n
Marsh, G. H., 251
Martin, J. C., 16, 604, 1587
Martin, R., 85
Martorana, S. V., 1559n
Marzulla, R., 1378
Mason, P., 368
Massaro, T. M., 1047
Massler, H., 1407n
Matasor, R., 88
Mathewson, A., 1156, 1157
Matthews, K. A., 367, 1437
Mayes, T., 748
McBride, S. P., 1154
McCarthy, J. T., 162, 598, 1513
McCaskey, A. S., 1157
McCaughey, M., 621, 655
McConnell, M. W., 719, 722
McCorkle, C. R., 289n, 1268n
McDaniel, D. L., 905
McDonald, S. J., 1033, 1048, 1337
McGillicuddy, M., 762n
McGuinness, A. C., 86, 1293
McHugh, W., 597
McKay, R., 1246
McKee, P. W., 598
McKendall, M., 75n
McKenna, J. A., 721
McKeown, J., 519
McMahon, M. J., 700n, 1363n
McMurtrie, B., 206, 1531
McNabb, S., 110, 160
McSherry, C., 1513
Mediation:
  collective bargaining, 296;
  Federal Mediation and Conciliation Service, 296;
  overview, 136–137
Medical leave, regulation of, 313–317

Medical privacy:
  drug testing, 269;
  preemployment examinations, 393
Medical screening of employees, 269–270
Medical services and research, laws regulating, 1288–1292
Medicare, 1397–1401
Meers, E., 823, 903
Meiklejohn, A., 1024
Melear, K. B., 82, 902
Melville, A. L., 1367
Menand, L., 718
Menard, A. P., 282, 499–500
Menkel-Meadow, C., 162
Mergers. *See also* Reductions in force:
  constitutional considerations, 587–594;
  contractual considerations, 579–587;
  statutory considerations, 594–595
Merges, R., 1358
Merico-Stephens, A. M., 1508
Merkx, G., 12
Metzger, W. P., 85, 613, 614, 616, 625, 718–719, 737, 1581n, 1583n, 1590
Meyers, D. K., 1589
Michaelson, M., 717
Milani, A. A., 1142
Military recruiting:
  homosexuals, military ban on, 442;
  institutional interference with, restrictions on, 1429–1432
Military veterans. *See* Veterans
Millard, R. M., 1251n, 1293, 1294
Miller, J., 1588
Miller, L. S., 903
Miller, N., 713, 1522
Miller, R. C., 190n, 437n
Milligan, R. B., 842n
Mingle, J. R., 604
Minicucci, R., 1533
Minimum contacts standard, 97–98
Minimum wage requirements, 305–311
Mink, B. P., 370
Mink, O. G., 370
Minor, J. T., 25, 665
Minow, M., 1332, 1386n
Mintz, B., 1522
Mintz, J., 719
Mitchell, B. C., 1196
Mitchell, M. R., 162
Mitten, M., 1157
Modesitt, N. M., 369
Moffitt, M. L., 162
Monaghan, P., 711
Money damages, 121–122
Montell, G., 543

Montgomery, V. W., 276n
Mooney, P., 33
Moorman, J., 1380
Mootness doctrine, 101–102
Moots, P. R., 88, 164, 1507
Morreale, J., 544
Morris, A., 517, 621
Mosely, D. M., 253
Moskow, M., 293
Motions to dismiss, 113
Mumper, M., 904
Mundel, D. S., 1517
Munsch, M. H., 1043
Murray, J. W., Jr., 603
Music and copyright protection, 1353
Myers, C., 623

N

Nahmod, S. H., 230n, 254
Nash, N., 14
NASPA. *See* National Association of Student Personnel Administrators
National Academy of Engineering, 1526
National Academy of Sciences, 1526
National Advisory Committee on Institutional Quality and Integrity, 1554
National Aeronautics and Space Administration, 1320, 1329
National Association for Women in Education, 737–738
National Association of College and University Attorneys (NACUA), 161, 253, 815–816, 1527
National Association of College and University Business Officers, 601, 905, 908, 909, 1380–1381, 1516, 1662
National Association of Independent Colleges and Universities, 1526
National Association of State Universities and Land-Grant Colleges, 1525–1526
National Association of Student Personnel Administrators (NASPA), 737–738, 1526, 1527
National Coalition for Women and Girls in Education, 942
National Collegiate Athletic Association (NCAA):
  antitrust laws, application of, 1566–1571;
  common law, application of, 1571–1573;
  external governance of higher education, role in, 29;
  federal civil rights statutes, application of, 1573–1581;

National Collegiate (*Continued*)
federal constitutional constraints, 1561–1564;
overview, 1560–1561;
state statutes regulating, 1564–1566
National Construction Law Center, 1611
National Direct Student Loan. *See* Perkins Loans
National Foundation of Arts and Humanities, 1425
National Institute of Education, 1267*n*
National Institutes of Health (NIH), 29, 1324–1325
National Labor Relations Act (NLRA):
bargainable subjects, 293–298;
certification, 287–293;
emotional distress claims, 293;
faculty bargaining unit eligibility, 491–492, 495–496;
organization, 287–293;
private institutions, collective bargaining at, 279–282;
public institutions, collective bargaining at, 286–287;
recognition, 287–293;
religious institutions, collective bargaining at, 282–286;
retaliation claims, 280, 328;
student workers, 302
National Labor Relations Board (NLRB):
higher education, jurisdiction over, 490–491;
unfair labor practice claims, 297–298
National Organization on Legal Problems in Education, 517
National origin discrimination:
in employment, 390, 408–411, 510–513;
in financial aid, 833–840;
Title VII, 318, 408–411
National Research Council, 1526
National Science Foundation (NSF), 1321:
financial aid programs, 1426;
financial disclosure policy, 1659;
grant programs, 1656;
research misconduct, regulation of, 1329
Naughton, J., 1134*n*
Nave, M. E., 1663
NCAA. *See* National Collegiate Athletic Association
Neff, E., 744*n*
Negligence:
alcohol consumption, injuries related to, 210;
assumption of risk, 202–203;
cocurricular activities, injuries related to, 206–210;

computer security, 198;
of employees, 334–337;
institutional liability for, 195–198;
negligent hiring, supervision, or retention of employees, 222–224;
off-campus instruction, injuries related to, 203–206;
on-campus instruction, injuries related to, 201–203;
outreach programs, injuries related to, 212–213;
premises liability, 198–201;
social activities, injuries related to, 206–210;
student suicide, 210–212;
of volunteers, 198
Neiger, J. A., 866, 1519
Nelson, F., 1294
Neumeg, R., 510*n*
"New GI Bill," 814
Newman, S., 690
Niccolls, C. S., 927, 1663
Nichols, D. H., 261
Nichols, J. E., 1155
Nicklin, J., 654*n*
NIH. *See* National Institutes of Health
NLRA. *See* National Labor Relations Act
NLRB. *See* National Labor Relations Board
Noncitizens, employment of, 317–320
Noncommercial solicitation on campus, 1236–1239
Noncompetition statutes, 1628–1632
Nondiscrimination. *See* Types of *discrimination*
Nonresidents
admissions, 777–778
financial aid, 825–833
Nordin, V. D., 86
Norman, E., 87
Norris, J. T., 624, 1522
NSF. *See* National Science Foundation
Nuss, E. M., 1044
Nuwer, H., 1154

O

Oberlander, J., 1514
Obesity as disability, 429–430
O'Brien, D., 425
O'Brien, M., 1519
O'Brien, T., 425
Obscenity in student press, 1107–1108, 1114
Occupational Safety and Health Act (OSHA), 303–305, 328
Occupational Safety and Health Administration:
enforcement role, 92, 303;

ergonomics standards, 305;
external governance of higher education, role in, 29
O'Connell, J. B., 160
O'Connor, E., 746
OCR. *See* Office for Civil Rights
O'Donnell, M. L., 1048
Off-campus injuries, institutional liability for, 203–206, 261
Office for Civil Rights (OCR):
admissions practices, complaints regarding, 760;
athletics, sex discrimination in, 1131, 1135–1136;
civil rights compliance, 1449–1450;
health insurance laws, enforcement of, 1402;
race neutrality, guidelines on, 802*n*;
sexual harassment, guidelines on, 948
Office for Good Clinical Practice Staff, 1318–1324
Office for Human Research Protections (OHRP), 1318–1324
Office of Information Technology, University of Maryland, 907
Office of Management and Budget (OMB)
conflicts of interest, 1659
financial aid policies, 1427
Office of Patent and Trademark, 1361
Office of Public Health and Science, 1324
Office of Research Integrity (ORI), 1329–1330
Officers, administrative authority of, 181–187
Ohasi, N., 1651
OHRP (Office for Human Research Protections), 1318–1324
Oleck, H., 1294
Olivas, M. A., 13, 82, 719, 779, 812, 826*n*, 839, 840, 905, 906, 1517
Oliveiri, D. J., 1167*n*
Olsen, F., 1533
Olswang, S. G., 291*n*, 536, 542, 603, 604, 902, 927, 1480, 1663
Olszowka, P., 1589
OMB. *See* Office of Management and Budget
On-campus injuries, institutional liability for, 201–203
O'Neil, R. M., 11, 83, 127, 163, 617, 621, 622, 654*n*, 655, 706, 717, 718, 719, 720, 721, 904, 907, 1023, 1047, 1517, 1518, 1522
O'Neill, J. P., 1294
Online Ombuds Office, 874

Open meetings laws, 1276–1280
Open records laws, 1281–1286
Oppenheimer, D. B., 466, 602
Oren, L., 953n, 956
Organizations, captive and affiliated:
  liability issues, 249–250;
  overview, 241–242;
  regulatory laws, application of, 246–248;
  state action issues, 248–249;
  structural problems, 242–244;
  taxation issues, 244–246
ORI (Office of Research Integrity), 1329–1330
Orleans, J., 894, 1157
OSHA. See Occupational Safety and Health Act
Osteen, C. M., 1415n, 1416
Ostrow, A. P., 1245
Oswald, J. D., 1044
Out-of-state institutions and programs, state regulation of, 1267–1272
Out-of-state students. See Nonresidents
Outreach programs, institutional liability for injuries related to, 212–213
Outsourcing, 1604, 1606–1608
Overland, M. A., 34
Overtime pay, 305–311
Overton, G. W., 250
Owen, K. Q., 370
Owensby, D. D., 1454

P

Page, R., 1017
Palfreyman, D., 87
Palmer, A. R., 134, 161
Palmer, C., 1518
Palmer, S., 903
Paludi, M. A., 465, 601
Paradis, L., 1513
Parent Loans for Undergraduate Students (PLUS), 814–815
Parker, J. W., 266
Parkin, L., 1514
Parsons, M., 1586
Part-time workers and contracts, 482–485
Pashman, S., 844
Patai, D., 717
Patents:
  animals, patentability of, 1358;
  infringement lawsuits, 1360;
  overview, 1355–1356;
  ownership of, 1358–1360;
  patentability requirement, 1356–1358;
  research collaboration, 1650–1652;
  sovereign immunity, 1360–1361

Paterson, B. G., 1045
Patry, W. F., 1513
Patti, C. M., 1401
Paulsen, M., 1153
Paulson, C., 1293
Pauly, M. V., 1514
Pavela, G., 83, 85, 113, 253, 746, 873, 907, 916, 927, 1042, 1044, 1046, 1096n, 1121
Payne, J. T., 477n
Pearlman, K., 1244
Pearson, T. C., 955
Peck, C. J., 263
Peer-to-peer file-sharing technologies and copyright law, 1340–1341, 1347–1350
Pell Grants, 814, 1433
Peltz, R., 1104
Performance management:
  background checks, 358–359;
  disciplinary actions, 360–362;
  employee evaluations, 359–360;
  performance improvement plans, 360;
  pre-hire issues, 357–359;
  promotions, 362–363;
  termination, 363–364;
Perillo, J. M., 580, 1592, 1596, 1662
Perkins Loans, 814, 849
Perritt, H. H., Jr., 365, 463, 601
Perry, M., 688
Peterson, A., 369
Peterson, B. G., 1044
Peterson, N., 1516
Phelps, W. G., 138n
Phillips, E., 369
Phillips, G. L., 1599n
Phillips, M. J., 88
PHS (Public Health Service), 1327
Picozzi, J. M., 981, 1043
Pieronek, C., 1131, 1157
PLUS (Parent Loans for Undergraduate Students), 814–815
Police, institutional relations with, 1206–1211
Polishook, I., 719
Porter, H. V., 1588
Porto, B. L., 400n, 1135n
Posner, R. A., 904
Post, D., 719
Postsecondary education, law of:
  academic custom and usage, 35–37;
  administrative laws and regulations, 31–32;
  case law, 37–40;
  common law, 32;
  constitutions, 30;
  evolution of, 9–22;
  external governance, 25–29;
  federal regulation, 1313–1406;
  governance, basic concepts of, 22–24;

  institutional contracts, 35;
  institutional rules and regulations, 35;
  internal governance, 24–25;
  international law, 32–34;
  law and policy, relationship between, 75–81;
  private institutions, legal rights in, 54–57;
  public-private dichotomy, 40–57;
  religion and public-private dichotomy, 57–75;
  scope of, 3–9;
  sources of, 29–40;
  state action doctrine, 42–54;
  statutes, 30–31
Postsecondary Education Convening Authority, 1294
Post-tenure review, standards and criteria for, 542–544
Powe, L. A., Jr., 908
Powell, M. B., 1084, 1087
Preemployment examinations and medical privacy, 393
Preemption, 304, 313, 1163–1164, 1297, 1368
Preer, J., 1519
Pregnancy discrimination, 412–414
Premises liability, 198–201
Prestage, J. L., 1521
Pretrial and trial issues:
  class action suits, 105–107;
  discovery, 107–108;
  evidence, 108–113;
  motions to dismiss, 113;
  summary judgments, 113
Preventive law, 144–150
Privacy Act of 1974, 1040–1041
Private institutions. See also Religious institutions:
  auxiliary enterprises, 1627–1628;
  collective bargaining at, 279–282;
  community access to campus, 1211–1213;
  disciplinary rules and regulations, 924;
  due process, 571–575;
  legal rights in, 54–57;
  sanctions, 988–993;
  state chartering and licensure of, 1258–1267;
  and student press, 1114;
  trustees, 174–181;
  zoning regulations, 1169–1173
Privilege:
  academic information, 699–706;
  attorney-client, 109–112;
  defamation, defense against, 218–219;
  psychotherapist-patient, 112–113

Procurement. *See* Purchases
Profit, J., 1588
Promissory estoppel, 345
Promotions of employees,
    362–363
Property taxes, 1184–1197
Prosser, W. L., 253, 1547
Protests. *See* Student protests
Przypyszny, J. R., 14, 81
Psychotherapist-patient privilege,
    112–113
Publication, academic freedom in,
    654–665
Public disclosure laws,
    1276–1280
Public figures, defamation of,
    1551–1553
Public Health Service (PHS),
    1327
Public institutions:
    auxiliary enterprises,
        1621–1627;
    collective bargaining at,
        286–287;
    community access to campus,
        1211–1213;
    constitutional due process,
        547–571;
    constitutionally based
        institutions, 1255–1258;
    construction contracts,
        1612–1615;
    disciplinary rules and
        regulations, 921–924;
    disciplinary sanctions,
        973–982;
    employment contracts,
        264–265;
    faculty personnel decisions,
        standards and criteria for,
        529–530;
    religious autonomy rights in,
        71–75;
    state actions by, 42–54;
    state authority over, 1250–1258;
    statutorily based institutions,
        1253–1255;
    statutory rights versus contract
        rights, 476–479;
    and student press, 1107–1114;
    suits against, 99–100;
    trustees, 172–174;
    unionization of employees,
        276;
    zoning regulations, 1167–1169
Public-private dichotomy:
    collective bargaining and,
        278;
    overview, 40–57;
    religion and, 57–75
Pulley, J., 1604
Purcell, E., 297
Purchases:
    construction contracts,
        1610–1618;
    of goods, 1599–1603;

of real estate, 1610;
of services, 1603–1610
Purver, J. M., 1600n

Q

Qualified immunity, 346–353
Qualified state tuition programs,
    1414

R

Rabban, D. M., 294, 367, 492,
    625, 719, 1664
Rabinowitz, R. S., 369
Racial discrimination:
    admissions, 758–762;
    employment, 389–391,
        406–408, 510–513;
    equal protection, 1451–1452;
    racial harassment, 408, 749, 958;
    reverse discrimination, 511–513;
    Section 1981. *See* Section 1981;
    Title VI. *See* Title VI;
    Title VII. *See* Title VII
Rahdert, G. K., 1515
Rains, R. E., 938
Ramares, A. K., 843n, 849n
Ramphele, M., 903
Rampino, K. J., 826n, 1199n
Ranney, J. T., 1157
Rap, R. E., 721
Rape, awareness of, 886
Ratcliff, J., 1534
RCRA (Resource Conservation
    and Recovery Act of 1976),
    1377–1378
Readmissions, 803–808
Real estate, purchases of, 1610
Reams, B., Jr., 18, 941
Reapportionment, 1205–1206
Reasonable accommodations
    of persons with disabili-
    ties, 391–393, 395–396,
    428–429
Recombinant DNA research,
    1324–1325
Recording Industry Association of
    America (RIAA), 1341,
    1349–1350
Redlawsk, D., 1047
Reductions in force:
    constitutional considerations,
        587–594;
    contractual considerations,
        579–587;
    overview, 579;
    preparing for, 596–597;
    statutory considerations,
        594–595
Regulatory laws and captive and
    affiliated organizations,
    246–248
Rehabilitation Act of 1973:
    administrative enforcement,
        1487, 1489, 1490n, 1493;

affirmative action, 1471–1472;
athletic teams and clubs,
    1140–1142;
computer access, 876;
employment discrimination,
    391–399;
enforcement remedies,
    1493–1501;
extraterritorial acts of
    discrimination, 1485–1486;
financial aid, 818;
obesity as disability, 429–430;
overview, 768–775, 959–972,
    1464–1469;
"program or activity," defined,
    1479–1481;
retaliation claims, 1483;
scope, 1472–1474;
unintentional discriminatory
    acts, 1474–1477
Reibstein, R. J., 252
Reidhaar, D. L., 85
Reisberg, L., 1032
Religion. *See also* Religious
    institutions:
    employment discrimination,
        433–435;
    public-private dichotomy and,
        57–75
Religious institutions:
    academic freedom in,
        714–716;
    collective bargaining in,
        282–286;
    employment discrimination in,
        456–462;
    faculty contracts, 485–490;
    government funds, use of,
        61–71, 840–842;
    religious autonomy rights in,
        59–61
Remedies:
    attorney's fees, 123–125;
    for breach of contract,
        1595–1597;
    contempt of court, 125–126;
    for employment discrimination,
        382–383, 501–510;
    exhaustion of, 103–105;
    injunctions, 122–123;
    for legal violations, 93;
    money damages, 121–122;
    overview, 121
Remis, R., 1122, 1157, 1296
Rescission of employment
    contracts, 267
Research:
    academic freedom in, 654–665,
        706–714;
    animal subjects, laws govern-
        ing use of, 1325–1329;
    confidentiality of findings,
        706–714;
    copies, fair use of, 1338–1339;
    federal regulation of,
        1318–1330;

human subjects, laws
governing use of, 1318–1325;
Institutional Animal Care and
Use Committees (IACUC),
1325–1327;
institutional review boards,
1319–1324;
misconduct, 1329–1330;
recombinant DNA, 1324–1325
Research collaboration:
antitrust law, application of,
1654–1655;
conflicts of interest, 1657–1662;
federal government incentives,
1655–1657;
patent law, application or,
1650–1652;
potentials and problems,
1640–1643;
research agreements,
1643–1650;
tax exemptions for research,
1652–1654
Reserve Officer Training
Corps (ROTC) programs,
1429
Residency discrimination in
admissions, 777–778
Res judicata doctrine, 118–121
Resource Conservation and
Recovery Act (RCRA) of 1976,
1377–1378
Respondeat superior doctrine,
222
Retaliation claims:
ADEA, 300;
False Claims Act, 328,
1404–1405, 1437;
federal civil rights statutes,
1482–1484;
First Amendment, 422–423,
588;
FLSA, 311, 328;
generally, 330, 373, 425, 612,
937–938, 955;
National Labor Relations Act,
280, 328;
OSHA, 303, 328;
Rehabilitation Act of 1973,
1483;
Safe Drinking Water Act, 328;
Title VI, 1483;
Title VII, 422–423;
Title IX, 388–389, 422–423,
424, 1483–1484;
Toxic Substances Control
Act, 328
Retirement incentive packages,
402, 432–433
Retirement income security,
regulation of, 311–313
Reverse discrimination, 511–513,
519–520
Reynolds, O. M., 1183*n*, 1244
Reynolds, W. L., 161
Rhodes, G. M., 206

RIAA. *See* Recording Industry
Association of America
Rich, B. A., 1296
Richards, R. F., 601
Richmond, D. R., 253, 981, 1513
Riesman, D., 15
Rigelhaupt, J. L., Jr., 1180*n*
Rigney, D. P., 905
Rinden, G., 210
Risk management:
hold-harmless and indemnifica-
tion agreements, 153–156;
liability insurance, 152–153;
overview, 150–151;
releases, 156–157;
risk avoidance versus risk
control, 151;
risk retention, 157;
risk transfer, 152–160;
suggestions, 150–151;
waivers, 156–157
Rizzo, M. J., 1250
Roady, C., 1516
Robert C. Byrd Honors
Scholarship Program, 814
Roberts, M., 1093
Roberts, T. E., 1244
Robinson, F., 110, 160, 1514
Robinson, J. H., 87, 722
Robison, W. L., 1665
Rodin, J., 1018
Roots, R., 849, 906
Rosenblum, J. E., 1665
Rosenblum, V., 597
Rosenhouse, M. A., 158*n*
Rosenthal, A., 1299
Rosenzweig, E. M., 1048
Rosner, S. R., 1153*n*
ROTC (Reserve Officer Training
Corps) programs, 1429
Rothstein, L. F., 16, 465, 601,
959*n*, 1513, 1519
Rotunno, N., 437*n*
Rowland, J., 303
Rubenstein, W. B., 465
Rubin, R., 1611
Rudolph, F., 40
Ruebhausen, O., 517
Ruger, P. H., 163, 516
Rules and regulations. *See* Disci-
plinary and grievance systems
Rush, S., 900, 1662
Russo, C. J., 366
Rutherford, L. H., 463, 1519
Rutledge, G. E., 1093, 1154
Ryan, C. S., 465
Rydstrom, J. F., 289*n*, 390*n*,
761*n*, 1051*n*

S

Sacken, D., 646, 1641
Safe Drinking Water Act, 328
St. John, E. P., 21, 906
Salary discrimination, 383–386,
517–521

Sales:
antitrust law, 1632–1633;
auxiliary enterprises,
1618–1628, 1639–1640;
entrepreneurial activities,
taxation of income from,
1634–1639;
noncompetition statutes,
1628–1632
Sales taxes, 1197–1199
Samels, J. E., 16, 604
Sanctions:
academic, at public
institutions, 982–988;
disciplinary, at public
institutions, 973–982;
hearings, 978–982;
notice, 978;
overview, 972–973;
private institutions, 988–993
Sanders, J. T., 1665
Sandin, R. T., 466, 601
Sandler, B. R., 465, 601
Sangree, 945
Santora, K. C., 145*n*
Satinover, T., 1510
Saunders, C., 1501
Savage, F. G., 164, 540
Scaraglino, P., 1403
Schaefer, H., 1293
Schaeffer, S., 1276*n*
Schechter, R. E., 1513
Schmid, W., 871
Schmidt, P., 1250, 1255, 1285
Schneider, A., 622*n*
Scholarships. *See* Financial aid
Schoonmaker, L. C., 463
Schopler, E. H., 296*n*, 978*n*
Schruers, M., 874
Schupansky, S. P., 1043
Schuster, J., 483
Schuster, J. H., 84
Schwartz, B., 1292
Schwartz, D., 1522
Schwartz, M., 230*n*
Schwartz, R., 305
Schweitzer, T. A., 938, 1044
Seal, R. K., 84
Searches and seizures in student
housing, 861–866
Seavey, W., 1547
Secretary of Education,
1532–1533, 1534, 1546, 1554,
1559–1560
Secretary of Health and Human
Services, 1397–1401
Section 504. *See* Rehabilitation
Act of 1973
Section 1981:
affirmative action, 820–821;
national origin discrimination,
408, 410;
1991 amendment to, 408;
racial discrimination, 389–391,
510–512, 760–762;
racial harassment, 408

Section 1983:
  damages, 121;
  equal protection, 1464;
  exhaustion of remedies, 104n,
    240–241, 576n;
  institutional liability, 230–241;
  personal liability, 346–357, 748;
  qualified immunity, 346–353;
  sex discrimination, 1464;
  sexual harassment, 953n,
    956–957, 959;
  sexual orientation
    discrimination, 436–437;
  state-created dangers, 353–357;
  statute of limitations, 102–103
Security. See Campus security
Sedler, R. A., 88
Seeber, R. L., 162
Seep, Ralph V., 1501n, 1505n
Segregation cases, 1451–1462
Seitz, J. L., 1373
Selden, W. K., 1588
Seldin, P., 370
Selingo, J., 895, 1377n
Sensenbrenner, R., 164
SEOG (Supplemental Educational
  Opportunity Grants), 814
Sergent, R., 1390n
Sermersheim, M. D., 163, 908,
  1513
Services, purchases of, 1603–1610
SEVIS. See Student and Exchange
  Visitors Information System
Sex discrimination. See also
  Sexual harassment:
  in admissions, 762–768;
  in athletics, 420–425,
    1127–1140;
  disparate impact claims,
    1135–1136;
  in employment, 386–389,
    513–515;
  overview, 411–412;
  pregnancy, 412–414;
  reverse discrimination, 519–520;
  salary, 517–521;
  Section 1983 claims, 1464;
  sexual orientation
    discrimination, 435–442;
  in standardized testing, 767;
  Title VII, 411–412;
  Title IX, 439
Sexual harassment. See also Sex
  discrimination:
  in employment, 414–420;
  First Amendment concerns,
    944–945;
  peer sexual harassment,
    749–752;
  same-sex, 437–438;
  of students by faculty
    members, 941–959;
  Title VII, 414–417, 419,
    943–945, 950;
  Title IX, 414, 749–752,
    943–954, 959

Shapiro, R. A., 1172n
Shapiro, S. R., 1002, 1239n
Sharp, L. A., 213, 415n
Shattuck, J., 1665
Shea, C., 1229
Shea, L., 1324, 1514
Shearer, P., 901
Shekleton, J. F., 182, 1293
Sherman, M., 690
Sherrill, J. A., 134, 161
Sherry, S., 1026
Shields, M. A., 273n, 1288, 1363n
Shiell, T. C., 1047
Shockley, P., 1650n, 1665
Shoop, R. J., 465, 601
Showalter, J. M., 129
Shropshire, K., 1156
Shubert, J. J., 82
Shuck, P. H., 1519
Shulman, J. L., 1115
Sidbury, B. F., 1048
Siegal, B., 1364
Siegler, L. C., 845
Siena, J., 1656
Silvergate, H., 1023
Silverman, L., 767
Silverstein, Z., 220
Simon, R., 717
Sims, J. C., 718
Sinder, J., 719
Sindler, A. P., 904
Sirefman, J., 162, 598
Sixteenth Amendment, 1301
Sizer, J. R., 1511, 1521
Skeel, D. A., Jr., 1589
Skitol, R. A., 1514
Sklansky, D., 1245
Skojec, S. A., 412n
Slaughter, S., 1643
Slivka, J., 1250
Smallwood, S., 302, 303
Smelser, N. J., 903
Smith, B. L., 210n
Smith, E. R., 882
Smith, F. S., 810
Smith, J. E., 200n, 213n, 876n
Smith, M. A., 894
Smith, M. C., 885, 909
Smith, S. G., 641, 720
Smith, T., 75n
Smith, W. M., 313
Smolla, R. A., 719
Snow, B. A., 81, 1157, 1307
Social activities, liability for
  injuries related to, 206–210
Soliciting and canvassing on
  campus, 1229–1230
Somers, P., 906
Song, J. K., 369
Sorensen, P. M., 252
Sorenson, G., 87
Sororities. See Fraternities and
  sororities
Sovereign immunity. See Immunity
Speech. See Academic freedom;
  First Amendment

Speiser, S., 213
Spille, H., 1294
Spitzer, R., 719
Sports. See Athletics teams and
  clubs
Sroka, S. L., 1461
Stafford Loans, 814
Stallworth, S. B., 85
Standardized tests
  copyright laws, application
    of, 1355
  sex discrimination, 767
Standards of judicial review,
  114–118
Standing doctrine, 100–101
Stanley, K. O., 866
Stanton, T. H., 1514
Stark, J. S., 85
State action:
  accreditation actions,
    1543–1546;
  by athletic associations and
    conferences, 1561–1564;
  of captive and affiliated
    organizations, 248–249;
  overview, 42–54
State governments:
  administrative procedure laws,
    1286–1288;
  medical services and research,
    laws regulating, 1288–1292;
  noncompetition statutes,
    1628–1632;
  open meetings laws,
    1276–1280;
  open records laws, 1281–1286;
  out-of-state institutions and
    programs, regulation of,
    1267–1272;
  postsecondary education,
    relationship with, 1247–1250;
  private postsecondary
    institutions, chartering and
    licensure of, 1258–1267;
  public disclosure laws,
    1276–1280;
  public postsecondary
    education, authority over,
    1250–1258;
  regulatory laws, 1273–1276;
  religious institutions,
    chartering and licensure of,
    1264–1267
Statutes of limitations, 102–103
Steadman, J. M., 1522
Steele, C. M., 903
Steinbach, S. E., 1381
Steneck, N. H., 1665
Stepka, D., 1394
Stern, J., 296
Sternberg, R., 797
Stevens, A. R., 1665
Stevens, E., 1046
Stevens, G. E., 253
Stewart, D., 1294
Stim, R., 1514

Stokes, J. W. D., 904
Stone, K. V., 162
Stoner, E. N., II, 129, 465, 916
Strickland, L. S., 1332
Strohm, L. C., 253
Strope, J. L., Jr., 1045
Strossen, N., 1048
Strout, E., 623
Student and Exchange Visitors
    Information System (SEVIS),
    898, 1316–1317
Student files and records:
    FERPA. See FERPA;
    Privacy Act, 1040–1041;
    state laws, 1035–1040
Student housing:
    off-campus housing, zoning of,
        1180–1183;
    regulations, 854–861;
    searches and seizures,
        861–866;
    Title VI, 856, 861;
    Title IX, 856
Student organizations:
    fraternities and sororities,
        1078–1096;
    institutional liability for acts of,
        191–192;
    mandatory student activity
        fees, 1058–1065;
    nondiscrimination principles,
        1065–1069;
    religious activities, 1069–1078;
    right not to join, 1056–1057;
    right to organize, 1050–1056;
    Title VI, 1067
Student press:
    advertising in, 1105–1106;
    general principles, 1096–1098;
    institutional regulation of,
        1100–1104;
    libel, 1108–1114;
    obscenity, 1107–1108, 1114;
    in private institutions, 1114;
    in public institutions,
        1107–1114;
    student fee allocations,
        1098–1100
Student Press Law Center, 1097n,
    1155
Student protests:
    in classroom, 1015–1017;
    criminal prosecutions,
        1010–1012;
    injunctions, 1010–1012;
    overview, 993–996;
    posters and leaflets,
        1012–1015;
    prior approval of, 1008–1010;
    "public forum" concept,
        996–1001;
    regulation of, 1001–1008
Student referenda, 1059–1061,
    1065
Student Right-to-Know Act,
    1122–1123, 1435

Students:
    academic freedom, 737–747;
    activity fees, 1058–1065;
    admission of. See Admissions;
    age of majority, 726–727;
    athletics. See Athletic teams
        and clubs;
    campus security. See Campus
        security;
    child care services, 899–900;
    codes of conduct, 913–916;
    community activities of,
        1239–1244;
    computers and. See Campus
        computer networks;
    conduct codes, 913–916;
    contractual rights, 727–737;
    with disabilities. See Students
        with disabilities;
    discipline. See Disciplinary and
        grievance systems;
    financial aid for. See Financial
        aid;
    fraternities and sororities. See
        Fraternities and sororities;
    health services, 888–893;
    housing. See Student housing;
    international students, services
        for, 896–899;
    with learning disabilities,
        admission of, 773–775;
    legal relationships with other
        students, 747–752;
    legal services, 900–901;
    legal status, 725–752;
    mandatory activity fees,
        1058–1065;
    organizations, 1050–1078. See
        Student organizations;
    peer harassment, 748–749;
    press of. See Student press;
    protests by. See Student
        protests;
    with psychiatric illnesses,
        disciplining, 924–927;
    records. See Student files and
        records;
    sexual harassment,
        749–752;
    suicide by, 210–212;
    taxation of, 1412–1415;
    voting by, 1199–1206
Students for Academic Freedom,
    746
Students with disabilities. See also
    Disabilities, persons with
    Disability discrimination:
    accommodations, requests for,
        965–972;
    concept of disability, 960–962;
    notice and documentation of
        disabilities, 962–965;
    overview, 959–960;
    psychiatric illnesses, discipline
        for students with, 924–927;
    services for, 893–896;

study abroad programs,
    participation in, 971
Student voting:
    canvassing and registering on
        campus, 1203–1205;
    elections, scheduling of,
        1202–1203;
    reapportionment, 1205–1206;
    registration, 1199–1202
Student workers:
    collective bargaining and,
        301–303;
    Title VII, 374
Study abroad programs:
    liability issues, 205–206;
    students with disabilities, 971
Sudia, D., 1122
Suggs, W., 1142
Suicide, institutional liability for,
    210–212
Sullivan, C. A., 601
Sullivan, K. M., 904
Sum, P. E., 1520
Summary judgments, 113
Sun, J. C., 136n, 1373
Sunstein, C. R., 908, 1048, 1327
Supplemental Educational
    Opportunity Grants (SEOG),
    814
Suspensions. See Sanctions
Sussberg, J. A., 1153n
Sweet, J., 1663
Swink, D. R., 261
Symbolic speech, 995

T

Tagg, J., 21
Tanaka, P., 847, 905
Tate, P. J., 14
Taxation:
    admission taxes, 1197–1199;
    amusement taxes, 1197–1199;
    audit guidelines, 1420–1423;
    of captive and affiliated
        organizations, 244–246;
    commercialization, 1419–1420;
    entrepreneurial activities,
        income from, 1634–1639;
    FICA withholdings, 1413–1414;
    fraternity and sorority houses,
        treatment of, 1188–1191;
    general tax concepts,
        1183–1184;
    gifts and contributions,
        1415–1416;
    intermediate sanctions,
        1410–1412;
    overview, 1406–1408;
    property taxes, 1184–1197;
    qualified state tuition
        programs, 1414;
    related entities, 1419–1420;
    research, exemptions for,
        1652–1654;
    sales taxes, 1197–1199;

Taxation: (*Continued*)
state and local taxes,
1637–1639;
of students, 1412–1415;
tax-exempt status, 1408–1410;
tuition tax credits, 1415;
unemployment compensation,
1414;
unrelated business income tax
(UBIT), 1416–1419,
1634–1637, 1653–1654
Tayler, C. W., 1588
Taylor, B. E., 250
Taylor, B. R., 602
Telecommuters, 261
Tenth Amendment, 1297
Tenure denials and terminations.
See also Faculty employment
decisions:
constitutional due process,
552–567;
judicial deference, 501–510;
overview, 531–542;
post-tenure review, 542–544;
remedies, 501–510;
Title VII, 506–508
Tepker, H. F., 131, 599
Termination of employment:
age discrimination, 364;
at-will doctrine, 262–263;
employee performance,
363–364;
wrongful discharge, 262–263
Terrell, M. C., 86
Terrorism:
federal response, 1330–1334;
war on, and academic freedom,
624
Tewksbury, D., 41
Thelin, J. R., 1115
Theuman, J. E., 1029n, 1369n,
1661n
Thielens, W., 717
Thigpen, R., 88
Thirteenth Amendment, 1305,
1307
Thomas, G., 13
Thomas, T. A., 390n, 410n
Thompson, A. J., 369
Thomsen, S. H., 313
Thomson, J. J., 719, 722
Thornton, S. R., 315, 368
Thrasher, F., 1382
Thro, W. A., 81, 823, 903, 1157,
1307, 1361
Tien, C., 903
Tierney, W. G., 13, 22, 25, 665
Tilles, E. A., 466
Title VI:
administrative enforcement,
1487–1492;
affirmative action, 782–783,
786–788, 795, 1471–1472;
athletic associations and
conferences, 1574–1577;
damages, 1483;

disparate impact claims,
1497–1498;
enforcement remedies,
1493–1501;
extraterritorial acts of discrimination, coverage of, 1484;
financial aid programs, 820,
822, 823, 825;
overview, 54, 1450–1462;
"program or activity," defined,
1479–1481;
racial discrimination, 758–761,
762;
racial harassment, 749, 958;
retaliatory acts, coverage of,
1483;
scope, 1472;
student housing, 856, 861;
student organizations, 1067;
unintentional discriminatory
acts, coverage of, 1474–1477
Title VII:
academic freedom, 702;
affirmative action, 443–449;
athletics coaches, 420–424;
attorney's fees, 510;
back pay awards, 390;
collective bargaining, 298–301;
consent decrees, 456;
damages, 121, 387, 1463;
disparate impact claims,
375–376, 380–381, 385–386,
388, 401, 404, 1135–1136,
1474, 1476–1477, 1497–1498;
disparate treatment claims,
375–377, 379–380, 382, 413;
extraterritorial application,
373;
national origin discrimination,
318, 408–411;
overview, 54, 374–383;
pregnancy discrimination,
412–413;
racial harassment, 408;
religious discrimination,
433–435;
religious institutions, 456–462;
retaliation claims, 422–423;
reverse discrimination,
511–512, 519;
salary discrimination, 385;
scope, 1474;
sex discrimination, 411–412;
sexual harassment, 414–417,
419, 943–945, 950;
sexual orientation
discrimination, 435–439;
state and local governments,
1304;
student workers, 374;
tenure denials, 506–508
Title IX:
administrative enforcement,
1487, 1489, 1490n;
admissions policies, 762–764,
767–768;

affirmative action, 782–783,
1471–1472;
alternative dispute resolution,
136;
athletic associations and
conferences, 1573–1574;
athletics coaches, 420–424;
athletic teams and clubs,
1127–1140;
damages, 121;
disparate impact claims, 388;
employment discrimination,
386–389;
enforcement remedies, 1489,
1493–1501;
extraterritorial acts of
discrimination, coverage of,
1484–1485;
financial aid programs,
817–818, 820, 822, 825n;
overview, 1462–1464;
"program or activity," defined,
1479–1482;
"receiving federal financial
assistance," defined,
1477–1479;
retaliation claims, 388–389,
422–423, 424, 1483–1484;
scope, 1472–1474;
sex discrimination, 439;
sexual harassment, 414,
749–752, 943–954, 959;
student child care, 899–900;
student health services,
889–890;
student housing, 856;
unintentional discriminatory
acts, coverage of, 1474, 1477
Tobin, E., 902
Tollett, K. S., Sr., 1461, 1520
Tort liability:
accreditation actions,
1549–1553;
alcohol consumption, injuries
related to, 210;
athletic injuries, 1147–1153;
cocurricular and social
activities, injuries related to,
206–210;
defamation, 217–222, 337–342;
educational malpractice,
213–217;
emotional distress, 224;
of employees, 332–344;
employees, negligent hiring,
supervision, or retention of,
222–224;
interference, 342–343;
invasion of privacy, 224, 342;
in loco parentis doctrine,
196–197;
negligence. See Negligence;
off-campus instruction, injuries
related to, 203–206;
on-campus instruction, injuries
related to, 201–203;

outreach programs, injuries related to, 212–213;
overview, 189–195, 332–334;
respondeat superior doctrine, 222;
student organizations, acts of, 191–192;
student suicide, 210–212;
study abroad programs, 205–206
Toxic Substances Control Act, 328
Tracy, J., 1244
Trademark, 1361–1368
Transcripts, withholding from debtors, 846–849
Traynor, M., 369, 721
Treatment law, 144
Treisman, P. U., 903
Trespass statutes, 1217–1229
Trial issues. *See* Pretrial and trial issues
Tribbensee, N. E., 77n, 212, 1043, 1049, 1386n, 1514
Tribe, L., 904
Trout, W., 1588
Trower, C. A., 470
Trubek, D. M., 95
Trustees:
authority of, 171–181;
overview, 171–172;
personal liability of, 188–189;
in private institutions, 174–181;
in public institutions, 172–174
Tuckman, H. P., 598
Turner, C., 20
Turner, M. G., 908
Tussey, D., 294n
Twenty-sixth Amendment:
scheduling elections, 1202;
voter registration, 1199;
voting age, 726

U

UBIT. *See* Unrelated business income tax
Ugland, E., 1246
Ultra vires doctrine, 169
Unemployment compensation:
Federal Unemployment Tax Act, 1414–1415;
generally, 325–327, 412n, 413
Unfair competition, regulation of, 1375–1376
Uniformed Services Employment and Reemployment Rights Act (USERRA), 330–332
Unintentional discriminatory acts, coverage by federal civil rights statutes, 1474–1477
Unions. *See* Collective bargaining
United Educators Risk Retention Group, 164
Universal Copyright Convention, 34

Unrelated business income tax (UBIT):
auxiliary enterprises, 1634–1637;
overview, 1416–1419;
research, exemptions for, 1653–1654
U.S. Citizenship and Immigration Services:
and foreign workers, 319;
immigration laws, enforcement of, 1314
U.S. Constitution. *See also specific articles and amendments:*
accreditation actions, application to, 1543–1546;
civil rights enforcement powers, 1304–1307;
commerce clause, 1268–1272;
commerce power, 1301–1304;
free exercise clause, 485–490;
overview, 1297–1299;
spending power, 1299–1301;
state sovereign immunity, 1307–1313;
supremacy clause, 836;
taxing power, 1301
U.S. Department of Agriculture, 1320, 1325, 1327
U.S. Department of Commerce, 1320
U.S. Department of Defense:
colleges operated by, 27;
external governance of higher education, role in, 29;
lobbying activities, restrictions on funds for, 1428;
procurement contracts, 1424
U.S. Department of Education (ED):
accreditation, role in, 1554–1559;
accrediting institutions, 1527;
Age Discrimination Act regulations, 1469–1470;
athletics, 1130–1131;
civil rights regulations, 1449–1450;
education associations, listed, 1525;
enforcement role, 92;
external governance of higher education, role in, 28;
Family Policy Compliance Office (FPCO), 1030, 1032, 1033;
financial aid programs, 1425, 1435–1436;
Freedom of Information requests, 1506;
human research subjects, laws governing use of, 1321;
lobbying activities, restrictions on funds for, 1428;
Office for Civil Rights (OCR). *See* Office for Civil Rights;

peer sexual harassment, guidance on, 749–750, 752;
race-exclusive scholarships, guidance on, 823, 825;
racial harassment, guidance on, 958;
Rehabilitation Act of 1973 regulations, 1464–1466;
sexual harassment, guidance on, 941–942, 953, 954–955;
student aid programs, eligibility requirements for, 835;
student records, 1029–1034;
Title VI regulations, 1451;
Title IX regulations, 1462–1463
U.S. Department of Energy, 1320
U.S. Department of Health, Education and Welfare (HEW), 1130
U.S. Department of Health and Human Services (HHS):
antiterrorism measures, 1333;
conflicts of interest, 1659;
external governance of higher education, role in, 28;
financial aid programs, 1425;
human research subjects, laws governing use of, 1318–1324;
research misconduct, regulation of, 1329–1330
U.S. Department of Health Education and Welfare (HEW), 796
U.S. Department of Homeland Security (DHS):
Bureau of Citizenship and Immigration Services (CIS), 898;
Bureau of Immigration and Custom Enforcement (ICE), 898;
external governance of higher education, role in, 28;
immigration laws, enforcement of, 1314
U.S. Department of Housing and Urban Development, 1320
U.S. Department of Justice (DOJ):
ADA enforcement, 1382;
antitrust investigations, 1548n;
athletic eligibility requirements, 1580–1581;
FCA, 1404–1405;
as plaintiff, 92;
student records, 1041
U.S. Department of Labor (DOL):
enforcement role, 92;
external governance of higher education, role in, 29;
family and medical leave, 314;
foreign workers, 318, 319–320;
Office of Federal Contract Compliance Programs (OFCCP), 406, 443–444;
Wage and Hour Division, 306

U.S. Department of State:
   exchange visitor program, 1316;
   and foreign workers, 318, 319;
   international students, role in
   regulating, 897-898
U.S. Department of the Interior, 27
U.S. Department of
   Transportation (DOT), 1321
U.S. Department of Veteran
   Affairs, 1321, 1426
U.S. Patent and Trademark Office,
   1357-1358
U.S. Student Association, 737-738
USA PATRIOT Act, 1330-1334
USERRA (Uniformed Services
   Employment and Reemploy-
   ment Rights Act), 330-332

V

Van Alstyne, W. W., 86, 615, 719,
   720, 722, 901
Vance, D., 1517
Van den Haag, E., 718
Van Der Werf, M., 1604
Vannelli, G. L., 1380
Van Tol, J. E., 602, 938
Van Wart, M., 365
Vargyas, E. J., 767, 820, 1463, 1497
Vazquez, C. M., 1361
Vento, C. S., 1274n
Veterans:
   employment of, 330-332;
   hiring preferences, 275
Viewpoint discrimination, 693,
   738, 901, 998, 1019, 1023,
   1024, 1026, 1028, 1054-1055,
   1075, 1078, 1099, 1243n,
   1444, 1448
Vinluan, R. A., 1080n
Virtual Magistrate Project, 874
Visas:
   for foreign workers, 318-319;
   for international students,
   897-899
Volokh, E., 908
Volunteers, negligence of, 198

W

Waelbroeck, S. E., 719, 722
Wagner, J. F., Jr., 392n, 1377n

Wagner, S. C., 412n
Waiver of contract rights,
   272-273
Waldo, C. N., 251
Walker, G., 1597n
Wallach, P. G., 1514
Wallick, R. D., 1518
Walton, S. J., 1155
Ward, J. A., 901
Ware, L., 1520
Wasserman, H. M., 1121
Wattley, M. A., 901
Weaver, S., 144
Weber, M. C., 465, 602
Weeks, K. M., 83, 163
Wegner, J. W., 1520
Weinstein, J., 631n
Weistart, J. C., 1157, 1589
Weitzner, D. J., 907-908
Welch, E. M., 369
Wellmann, J., 906
Wells, M., 230n
Wergin, J., 1534
West, J. P., 276n, 365
West, M. S., 602
Westman, D. P., 369
Wetherington, G. T., 721
Whistleblower protections,
   327-330, 1274n, 1329, 1437
White, L., 1434
White, R. H., 466
Whitehead, K. D., 1518
Whitman, R. S., 455
Whitten, A. D., 253
Wiggins, E. C., 721
Wilcox, J., 16
Wilhelm, S., 1045
William D. Ford Direct Loan
   Program, 815
Williams, D. T., 22
Williams, E., 437n
Williams, J. B., IV, 1520
Williams, P., 1157
Williams, R. E., 906
Williams, W. M., 905
Wilson, J. B., 717, 902
Wilson, R., 17, 470, 652, 684n,
   903, 1161, 1521
Winston, G. C., 14
Witten, R. E., 599
Wolverton, B., 1283
Wong, G. M., 1156, 1157, 1560

Woodcock, R. L., 906
Woods, G. W., 1404
Wooster, A. K., 314n, 389n, 392n,
   1381n
Workers' compensation:
   athletes and, 1122;
   employees and, 320-325, 1402
"Work made for hire" doctrine,
   1344-1346
Wright, B., 13
Wright, T. W., 86
Wrongful discharge, 262-263
Wu, T., 873

Y

Yale-Loehr, S., 1515
Yamada, D. C., 369
YMCA and YWCA and Title IX
   issues, 1462
Young, D. P., 902
Young, K. E., 1588
Young, S., 1589
Youngers, J., 1522
Ytreberg, D. E., 1050n

Z

Zamansky, J., 1514
Zeiner, C., 1610
Zelin, J. E., 296n
Zimbalist, A., 1115
Zimmer, M. J., 601
Zipp, E. K., 400n
Zirkel, P. A., 83, 1043, 1045
Zitter, J. M., 917n, 925n, 1171n
Zoning and land use regulation:
   amendment of ordinances,
   1177-1178;
   off-campus housing, 1180-1183;
   overview, 1167;
   private institutions and,
   1169-1173;
   property owners, rights of,
   1178-1180;
   public institutions and,
   1167-1169;
   special exceptions, 1173-1177;
   variances, 1173-1177
Zulkey, E., 342
Zupanec, D. M., 854n, 855n,
   1229n